CW01656216

ISBN: 978-0-9556863-9-9
Publisher: Fundays Enterprises Ltd (R) 2010
Fundays Enterprises Ltd (R) Registered Office:
Somserset House 40 – 49 Price Street,
Birmingham, B4 6LZ

Foreword

My interest in Confucius began many moons ago but like most people I knew very little about him. I read the *Analects* when I was teaching in China but these aphorisms were not easily accessible without context, as such, the wonders of such a brilliant and enlightened mind did not fully register with me.

Then a few years ago my interest in Confucius was rekindled and this time I decided to read about his life and times. I am particularly indebted to two books Shigeki Kaizuka's '*Confucius His Life and Thought*' and H G Creel's '*Confucius and the Chinese way*'. Through them I received a greater appreciation of Confucius' thought and era.

Confucius lived in a most bloody period of Chinese history, plagued by many inter-state wars and great political intrigue. The power of the Zhou Emperor had become purely nominal. Real power lay in the hands of the states and their rulers. And in turn much of the power of the Princes of these states was usurped by noble families. Thus for example in Confucius' own state of Lu, de facto power was in the hands of the 'Three Huan', three families descended from an earlier Duke Huan of Lu.

Under such a dangerous and fickle period it is quite amazing to think how Confucius, with his radical 'Humanitarian' ideas and constant criticism of the rulers was nonetheless held in high regard and great affection by them - though he was never offered high governmental position. However, his disciples were in great demand and employed by the rulers as they were extremely accomplished, trustworthy and loyal - traits which were highly sought after during such capricious times.

The most wondrous thing about Confucius is that he was not a prophet and never lay claim to being one. He did not come preaching any particular religion from any particular god. He was far more interested in the *physical* plight of his fellow Man and not interested in discussing Heaven and the life hereafter. For Confucius it was incumbent upon the *Ruler* to look after and promote the well-being of his citizens. His duty was that akin to a father's to his children.

Confucius believed that the nobility of a person did not lay in the accident of birth but in Learning and Self-cultivation. The 'princely man' – the gentleman or in Confucius' word '*Junzi*' is the Ideal Man that all should aspire to, through learning, such as: *Xin* – honesty and trustworthiness; *Shù*- selflessness and faithfulness towards all friends, family and strangers*; Lǐ* - ritual and the norms of proper social behavior as taught by fathers, village elders and government officials; *Yì* – the ability to be righteous and act in a just manner*; and Xiào* – love for one's family, parents and country, which he believed lay at the root of Humaneness; *Jén* – practice of benevolence and humanity.

All the above were underpinned on the guiding principle of ***Reciprocity*** - *never do anything to anyone else that you wouldn't want them to do to you.*

I do not wish to make Confucius out to be some infallible 'Divine Soul' to be revered as a god. He was a *Man* and far from being perfect and never lay claim to the 'Ultimate Truth.'

Confucius thought, true knowledge consisted not in a blind acceptance of, but in a critical study of traditions concerning the earlier dynasties. *'If a man enquires into the past in such a way as to acquire knowledge about the present, he is a fit person to become a teacher of others'* thus Confucius was alluding to adopting the process of inference - a knowledge of the traditions of the past coming to inform knowledge of the present.

In my humble way I have tried to make his thoughts more accessible to the slightly curious reader and hope it will prompt him/her to discover more about one of the greatest but much neglected (in the West) minds of history whose words I believe still resonate with the reader of today,

For the Lady who my inspiration shall remain forever
A most radiant generous wonder
Bibi Ghulam Raza
My Mother

A Pearl of Wisdom

Confucius

Q Shah

List of Characters

Confucius
Confucius' Mother
Wang Yi (friend)
Shu-sun (Premier of Lu)
Viscount D'an
Duke Chao
Kung Wei (The Crown Prince of Lu)
Chao-po (A nobleman of Lu)
Tsang Ch'en (A nobleman of Lu)
Chi P'ing-tzu (The de facto ruler of Lu)
Chung Li (A retainer of P'ing-tzu)
Tzu Chia-tzu (A retainer of Duke Chao)
Retainer (of the Shun-sun family)
Passer-by
Landlord
Music Master
Duke Ching of Ch'i
Prince (Duke Ching's son)
Tzu-lu (A disciple of Confucius nine years Confucius' junior)
Kong Li (Confucius' son)
Min Sun (A disciple – fifteen years Confucius' junior)
Jan Yung (A disciple - twenty years Confucius' junior)
Jan Po-niu (A disciple)
Jan Chi'iu (A disciple)
Kung-Hsi Hua (A disciple)
Duke Ding of Lu
Yang Hu (a Steward of Chi P'ing-tzu)
Chi Huan-tzu (son of Chi P'ing-tzu and later de facto ruler of Lu)
Chung-liang Huai (a Steward of Chi P'ing-tzu)
Huang-tzu (Chi Huant-tzu' cousin)
Yang Yueh (Yang Hu's cousin)
Lin Ch'u (a former guard of Chi P'ing-tzu)
Yen Hui (A disciple – 30 years Confucius' junior)
Tzu-Kung (A disciple – thirty-one years Confucius' junior)
Chi Kang-tzu (son of Chi Huan-tzu and later the de facto ruler of Lu)
Ssu Ma Niu (A disciple – a nobleman of Song)

Duke Ling of Wèi
Nan-tzu (wife of Duke Ling)
Huan Zhou (the head of the K'uang mob)
Lady
Duke of She
Kung Yu (Minister and de facto ruler of Wèi)
Duke Ai of Lu
Tzu-chang (A disciple – a native of Chen - forty-eight years Confucius' junior)
Tzu-hsia (A disciple – a native of Wei - forty-five years Confucius' junior)
Yen Lu (Yen Hui's father)

Contents

孔夫子
Kǒng fū zǐ

天命
tiānmìng

(Act I) - Heaven's Mandate

'To rule justly fairly and wisely in the interests of the people'

Sān Huáng Wǔ Dì Jì[1]

In the mists of time
Heaven entrusted its Mandate
in the hands of the Three August Ones Divine[2]
The Heavenly King[3]
The Earthly King[4]
The Human King[5]
who used their magical powers to better their people's state.

Their reign was built on virtues, lofty
ushering a great period of peace and harmony.
Following the example of their Sovereignty most Heavenly
The Five Sage Emperors did rule most morally[6]

The Yellow Emperor (黄帝)
Zhuanxu (顓頊)
Emperor Ku (帝嚳)
Emperor Yao (堯)
Emperor Shun (舜)
As did Yu, founder of the Xià Dynasty

---

[1] Mythical Period of the 3 Heavenly and five Sage Emperors
[2] (三皇殿) Sān Huáng
[3] (天皇) Tiān Huáng
[4] (地皇) Dì Huáng
[5] (泰皇 or 人皇) Tài Huáng
[6] According to the Records of the Grand Historian (史記 - Shǐjì)

The Xià Dynasty (夏朝)

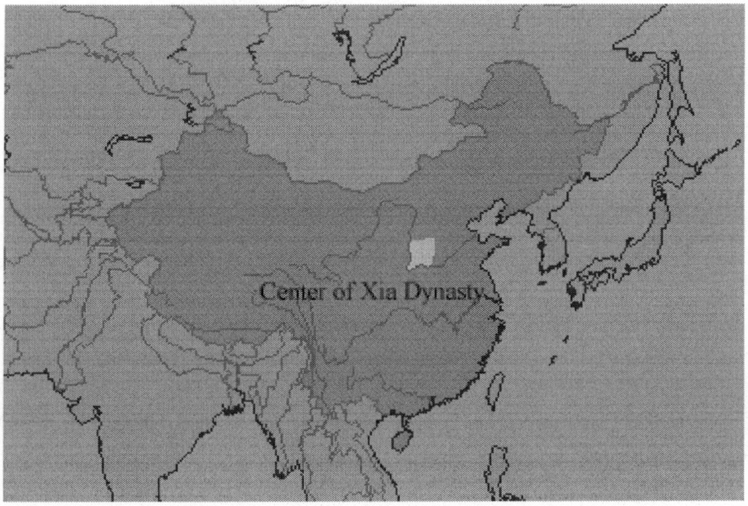

For three centuries, 2100 to 1800 B.C.
Heaven's Mandate remained with the Xià Dynasty
until King Jie assumed power in pomp and glory.
A tyrant he mistreated his people most miserably.
During the last years of his reign
Heaven's anger was made plain.
Ice formed during the summer mornings
and frosts through July occurring.
Heavy rain toppled many buildings.
With hot and cold weather disorderedly arriving
and crops failing,
time on King Jie's decadent rule was finally closing.

Mo Xi, the beautiful but amoral concubine
with her sexual prowess did King Jie entwine.
She enjoyed music and wine,
with a penchant for jugglers
and female singers,
she had King Jie made, a lake of wine.
Once finished, she commanded 3000 men to drink dry the lake,
and when all drowned she did cachinnate

Thus it was in 1675 B.C.
that Heaven terminated its Mandate with the Xià dynasty,
and invested in Cheng T'ang
of the tribe of Shāng,
Who defeated King Jie's army
at the battle of Mingtiao under a thunderstorm most heavy.

Shāng Dynasty (商朝)[7]

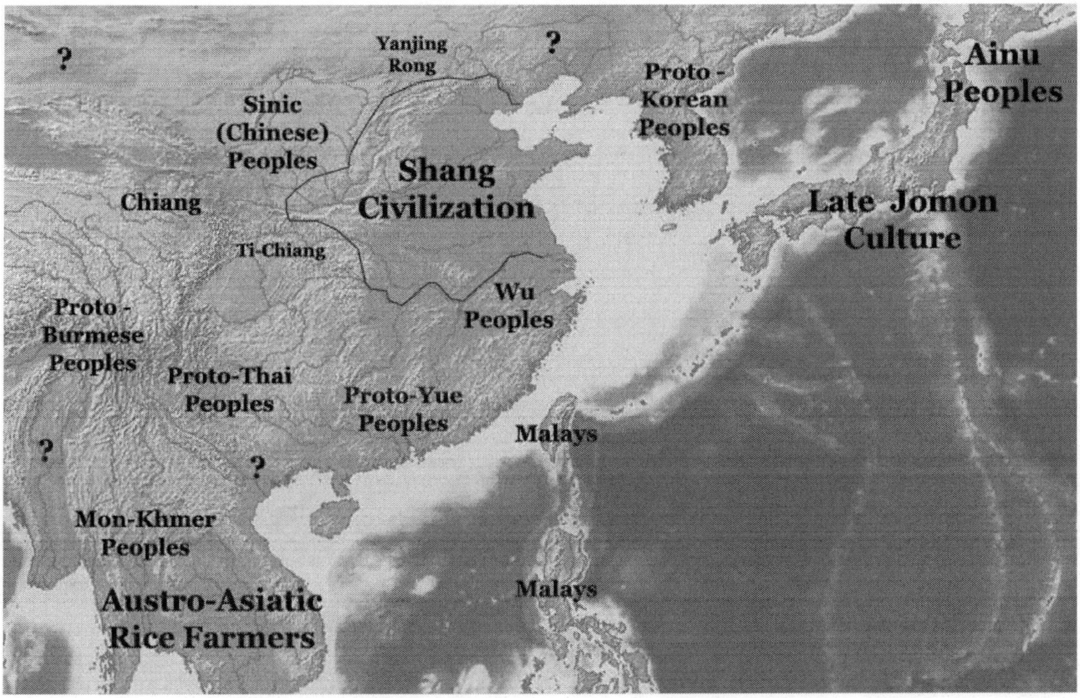

King T'ang was a man of great wisdom and virtue,
in the second year of his reign
a drought of 5 years duration came.
Many a parent, to barely survive
had to sell their children in order to keep alive.
During this period King T'ang had many a golden coin made
and to the poor who had their children sold he had paid,
so they could buy them back again.
Tang prayed at Sanglin, promising that if it did not rain,
he would sacrifice himself to the God in charge of Rain.
Finally, the Heavens did open and rain,
For T'ang, was a man of great wisdom and virtue!

[7] Also known as Yīn Dynasty (殷代) 1766 BC and 1122 BC

Like the Xià before,
the Shāng after 700 glorious years could hold power no more
falling prey to the evils of Excess and Debauchery
reaching the height of Decline and Depravity
with the last Shāng King, Di Xin[8] who ruled most ignominiously.

However it had not always been this way,
in the early part of Di Xin's rule,
for being quick-witted and quick-tempered gained he a name,
extremely intelligent and shrewd,
he was strong enough to hunt wild beasts with his bare hands they say.

In his later years, Di Xin came under the influence of his wicked wife Daji
and was given to drinking, women and a lack of morality,
and wicked deeds of extreme cruelty
preferring these pursuits to the proper governance of the country,
ignoring almost all affairs of state.
he hosted festive orgies in number great
and songs with erotic lyrics he enjoyed to create[9]

Di Xin had on the Palace grounds made
A Meat Forest and a Pool of Wine
big enough for several canoes to pass at the same time
with inner linings of polished stones oval shaped
Which allowed the entire pool to be filled with wine
With a small island in the middle planted with many a tree
with branches of roasted meat skewers hanging over the pool.
Di Xin, and his courtiers for amusement drifted on canoes in the pool.
When taken by thirst, they reached down into the pool and drank the wine.
When they hungered, they reached up with their hands and ate the roasted meat.
Further to please Daji
the 'Cannon Burning Punishment' of agony
was he the creator.

---

[8] Also known as Zhou
[9] According to Sima Qian

A large, oil covered bronze cylinder
And on burning charcoal placed.
To walk on top were the prisoners made.
As the cylinder did heat,
the prisoners were forced to shift their feet
to avoid the burning heat.
Further, the oil made it difficult for the prisoners to on top remain.
They were thus forced to dance in fear and agony,
Screaming in prolonged pain,
while at the tortured dances did laugh Di Xin and Daji.
The prisoners would fall
and burn to death on the charcoal.
While, Di Xin and Daji
after watching such torture would get aroused highly.

In order to fund Di Xin's lifestyle of licentious luxury
taxes were implemented most heavily.
The civilians suffered greatly,
and lost all hope for the Shāng dynasty.
Di Xin's brother Wei Zi tried to persuade
Di Xin to change his ways, but was rebuked sternly.
His uncle Bi Gan similarly him remonstrate,
but Di Xin had his heart ripped out for curiosity
to see how looked the heart of a sage.

Angered by the breaking of the covenant
Heaven, eventually made its wrath manifest in an instant
by investing it to King Wen and his son Wu of the Zhōu dynasty,
When at the Battle of Muye, ended the rule of the Shang dynasty.
Di Xin gathered all his treasures around himself in the Palace,
and committed suicide by setting fire to his Palace.

The Zhōu Dynasty (周朝)

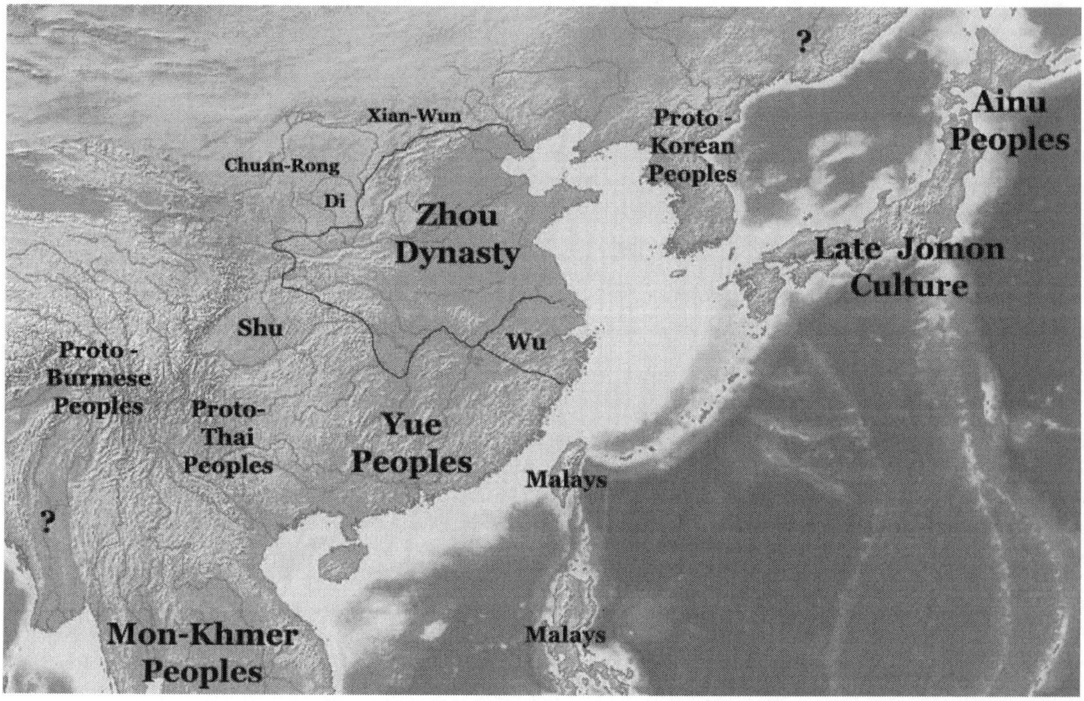

The Zhōu was the longest of all dynasties to reign,
From 11th century BC to 221 BC in power they did remain.
In the beginning there were the Kings Wen and Wu[10]
morally upright rulers whom all the citizens did venerate.
The Way[11] did they originate,
which long forgotten in Confucius' time he tried to renew.

[10] 文武

[11] Dào 道 the perfect Way to live and conduct one's life in accordance to the precepts of virtue, justice, respect, and sincerity towards others, it implies adherence to rules of propriety.

The nine centuries of Zhōu dynasty
was also a time of profound change in Chinese society.
The first kings of Zhōu enfeoffed their family with many a large domain
that later independent kingdoms became
Thus over time, the central government lost its authority,
As the age of enfeoffment disintegrated
And the kings of Zhōu, once so venerated
lost their central position as Guardians of Heavenly Sovereignty
And were challenged often by many a feudal lord
who overtook the leadership of the Chinese world.

Eastern Zhōu

Spring and Autumn Period[12]

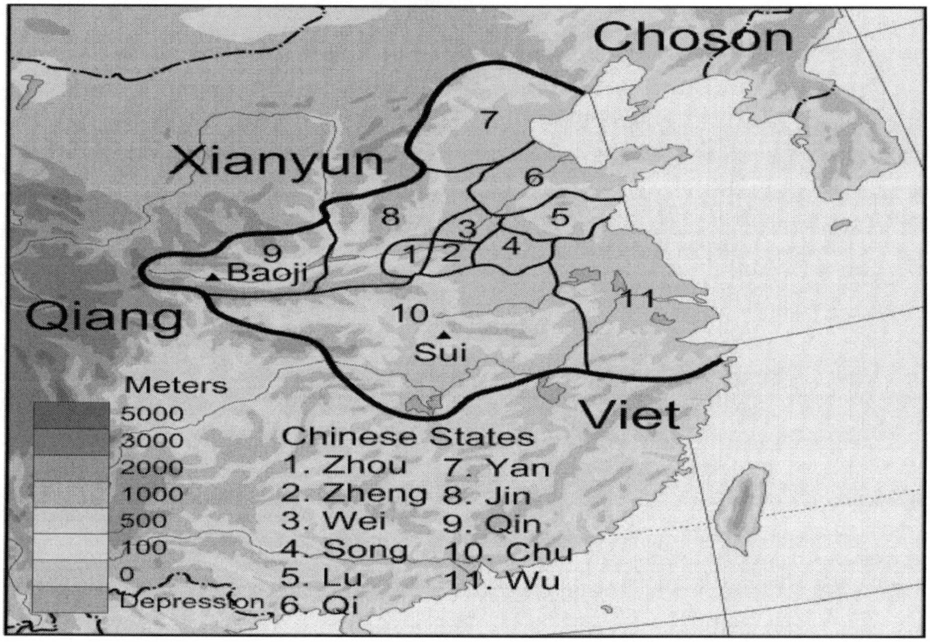

Northern 'barbarians' overran the Western Zhōu around 771 BC
and conquered their capital city.
The Zhōu king was killed, but his son, and heir Xuan Jiu did flee,
and established his government in Luoyi.[13]

This began the Eastern Zhōu period.
And was divided into the Spring and Autumn period,
Over 25 emperors reigned over the Eastern Zhōu Dynasty,
It was a time full of change, turbulence and uncertainty
marked by the scramble for hegemony,
There were over 140 states which led to the emperor's loss of authority

According to recorded history,
It was a period ravaged by over 480 wars and conspiracy
territory shifted back and forth, invasions took place frequently,
alliances formed and dissolved with astonishing rapidity.

[12] Ch'un-ch'iu (春秋) (770 BC - 481 BC) - So called following the seasonal recordings of the official chronicle of the Lu Court

[13] Luoyang in present day Henan Province

Powerful states developed quickly
and began to annex weaker ones eventually
Until Five overlords declared their hegemony
during this period in succession:
the Huangong of the Qi State,
Xianggong of the Song State,
Wengong of Jin, Mugong of the Qin State
and Zhuangwang of the Chu nation

Though the Spring and Autumn period was one of great danger and uncertainty,
Nonetheless, it was a time of supreme prosperity in economy,
Seeing an energetic flourishing of science, culture and thought in Chinese history.
The Zhōu was the time of the hundred schools of philosophers and thinkers of stature
establishing the rudiments of Chinese philosophy, ethics, political theory, and culture
The three most important, being Daoism,
Confucianism, and Legalism.

In the latter part of the Spring and Autumn period,
two states, Wu and Yue contended for overall power.
Previous to this period,
the league of states of the central plain, with Qin as their leader,
had been harried by the raids and inroads to the north by Ch'u,[14] constantly
the kingdom said from alien tribes to have originated, grew powerful rapidly,
Since frontal defence was far from easy against Ch'u,
the allied states tried to attract into their camp the newly risen kingdom of Wu.[15]

The policy of the League was to incite Wu to engage with Ch'u,
and thus weaken the force of the latter's northern infiltrations
into their nations

[14] Modern day Wu-han area
[15] with its capital situated in modern day Suzhou

Hu-Liang Ho of Tsou[16]

Qin convened the allies of the central plain, and inviting the prince of Wu,
held an inter-state conference, with the plan of drawing up opposition to Ch'u.

It was decided at the convention
that in order to secure this vital line of communication,
the small aboriginal state of Pi-yang was to be taken,
Lu also supplied troops under its prince Duke Hsiang for the allied force.
However, this small fort,
which seemed hardly worth taking the effort,
was in fact so stoutly defended
that its capture became drawn out contrary to expected.

An attempt to storm the fort
came to naught.
The gate of the fort was flung open suddenly,
the allied warriors all wishing to distinguish themselves on the battlefield,
vied with one another to be the first to take the field;
watching carefully for the moment, the gatekeeper slammed the gate suddenly.

Enter.... Shu-liang Ho
of Tsou!
A tall, broad, strong sort
calm brave and bold
in the midst of the warriors so panicked and startled,
he was not the least unmettled,
grasping the wooden bar
prized one of the leaves of the gate from its hinges apart,
held it up while the allied warriors made good their escape.
A remarkable feat of strength to wrench open the gate
and hold it up single-handed whilst others made good their escape!

His deed of valour and prowess
reverberated throughout Lu and the allied states to all impress
The general of the Lu,
was head of the noble clan of Meng-sun, named Meng Hsien-tzu,
renowned for engaging to the services of his family
knights distinguished for their bravery
thus employed the Shu-liang Ho to the service of his family.

---

[16] 563 BC Confucius' father

Ch'i's Invasion of Lu[17]

Lu was raided by her powerful northern neighbour Ch'i,
which formerly held hegemony of the central plain,
and throughout the Ch'un-ch'iu period it did remain
a menacing and formidable enemy.

The force of Ch'i was split in two, one laid siege to Fang,
the seat of the Tsang-sun an illustrious Lu family.
A relieving force was despatched from the capital city,
but was afraid to approach too near the fort of Fang.

One of those holding Fang was Shu-liang Ho,
who had command of a detachment of the defending company.
Taking counsel with the Tsang family,
he advised the head, Tsang-sun Ho
to leave the beleaguered fort,
and so, with the young stalwarts of the clan, and 300 knights as escort,
he the head of the House, Tsang-sun Ho did guide,
through the lines of the besieging force
under the cover of night,
the troops reached the camp of the relieving Lu force,
and immediately after Shu-liang Ho
retraced his steps, attacked the investing army and returned to Fang once more.

Thus was Confucius' father,
who in sheer physical strength yielded to no other
with boundless courage and valour,
but was not born of reckless nature,
he was of cool discrimination with a staunch sense of duty.
In times of war, a calm courageous loyal warrior,
whilst in times of peace, firm of will and integrity.

[17] 556 BC

(Act II) - The Birth of Confucius

Confucius was born in 551 B.C.
in the village of Tsou, in the state of Lu
in the city of Qu'fu
Of noble ancestry,
K'ung Fangshu was his early ancestor
of a king of Sung, a ninth-generation ancestor
K'ung was the father of Pohsia,
who was Shuliang Ho's father.
The ancestors of Confucius before K'ung Fangshu
held no positions high or mighty,
but K'ung Fangshu
became the administrator of a county
of Lu.

His father was over sixty four and his mother only fifteen when they did marry.
Confucius's father, already had two wives, nine daughters, and one disabled son.
But he longed to have a son who would his family's name carry
So Ho married Cheng-tsai in the hope that she would bear him a son.

When Cheng-tsai and Ho did not have a baby,
Cheng-tsai went to the sacred Nich'iu Hill[18]
to pray for a son to her life fulfil.
In answer to her prayer Confucius was born
However, his father died three years after Confucius was born,
leaving the family in poverty.

He was brought up by his mother most lovingly,
and he in turn adored her equally
From an early age, Confucius, a great desire of learning did display,
and veneration for the ancient laws of his country.
At fifteen he enrolled at the village school and devoted his life to study
He was married at 19 some say
to a young girl named Qi Quan
who bore him two daughters and one son,
but divorced four years later that he might have more time for studies
and the performance of his public duties.

---

[18](Ni) Qui = hill

Born in humble circumstances he acquired many a skill for a living.
And upon reaching manhood,
many a petty job undertook,
from book-keeping to livestock caring.
He worked as a market keeper,
then took care of parks and livestock as a farm worker.
When he was 20, he worked for the district governor.
He was keeper of the Lu granary and supervisor of the fields later,
Even though the fortunes of his family had declined, he was no commoner.

At 15 Confucius entered the community school run by the village Elders
Where he acquired knowledge of the different religious ceremonies
connected with the worship of the clan deities,
practised in the community's year-round activities.

Social convention dictated the highest esteem for the Elders
The etiquette of the banquet was held in association with religious festivities
to honour the clan deities
in country communities

In the districts, the basis of the ritual in the young lay
the elders at feasts were invited to stay,
and of bygone events were asked to recount fully
told in the oral traditions of the community.
Such, in fact was one of the aims of the ceremony.

The aims of the elementary study
was to impress upon the young most earnestly
the etiquette of respectful service towards the elderly
and to learn from them the community's history
in brief, the purpose of education was quite simply
to enable them to grow into useful adult members of the community.

Confucius was a most avid learner
who shone amongst his peers with his intelligence and endeavour.
An amiable young soul
loved by peers, Elders and all.
Excelling in his elementary schooling
he was sent to the state capital Qu'fu for further learning
On 'The Documents' and 'The Odes'
Of Ancient Zhōu's

The Odes contained many a verse of eulogy
in honour of Kings Wen and Wu
who the Shang kingdom did overthrew
and established Zhōu's rule for many a century.

The Odes[19] were of three in variety
First the Hymns of Praise - the libretti
music sung to the accompaniment of an orchestra
and offered at festivals to honour
the spirits of the August founders of Zhōu.
Then, formal songs sung on the occasion of feasts in honour
of stately guests at the court of Zhōu
And the 'State Airs' lastly,
words of music offered to Zhōu
from various vassals of its territory.
There were a number of blind musicians at the Zhōu Court Orchestra
who would give special performances of the Odes.

Orally were passed the words of the Odes
from father to son and to pupil from master.

A group of Music Masters were sent from the Zhōu Court
to the Lu Court
in order that the Zhōu culture
remained true even in the provinces of the Empire.

Confucius having studied ritual, procedure and local history
then went to University in Qu'fu,
the metropolis of Lu,
to study the Odes under a group of blind court musicians
and soon became a most accomplished of musicians,
with assiduous study.

The Music Master was a hereditary position
and was treated with some contempt by the nobility
who had little love for commoners whom they viewed most lowly.
Confucius however treated the Musician
with great respect and dignity
due to a Master most praiseworthy.

[19] The lines of Odes consisted of 4 monosyllabic characters, with the final character rhyming, and were intoned to the accompaniment of musical instruments, thus even when read without the orchestra they retained a smooth-flowing rhythm forcing the reciter to vary the modulation.

Thus on the occasion of a visit by a Music Master,
Confucius pointed out *'the steps are here',*
at the bottom of the staircase, as he was stepping to be seated,
with these words *'the chair is here'* him he so guided.

'The Documents' in Confucius' time
were mostly of the Duke of Zhōu's writing.
The structure was not based on any determined length of line
nor did the lines rhyme,
the words being difficult to commit to memory were put to writing
on bamboo and other wood,
cut into strips, a number of which were then together put
and tied by thongs of leather,
and upon which with the stylus' incision was carved each and every character

Such documents were inconvenient to preserve and read,
consequently, restricted was their range of circulation.
Archived were they in the offices of the 'Grand Historian'[20]
of the Zhōu Royal Court
and in several state capitals they could be sought.
Confucius at the Archivist of Lu, the Documents did learn to read.

Further, various rituals and procedures Confucius did study
from the officials who presided over many a ceremony.

Back in Lu, Confucius became an official of some standing,
Taking part in the celebrations at the state ancestors temple.
Asked he questions of the assistants of the Master of the Temple
concerning each and every detail of the procedure,
Thus insultingly was he described the great ritual scholar
son of a country commoner.

'Can any son of Tsou[21] know the ritual?'
for he always asks about everything when he goes into the temple'
However, unperturbed remained he from these arrogant personalities.
Finally, from the officials of the Board of Ceremonies
did Confucius complete of ritual procedure his training.

---

[20] Also known as the 'Internal Historian'

[21] A derogatory term used by the urban nobles residing in the Lu capital Qu'fu for the son of a military knight living in the country

The Government of the Sage Ministers 538 - 523 B.C.

During Confucius' formative age
it was the time of the Ministers most sage ....
The wise Tzu Chan the Cheng Premier,
a state of the central plain
Shu Hsiang, in Qin the head of the confederacy of states of the plain
was an extremely influential political adviser.
And, Yen Ying, a great scholar and first statesman,
from Ch'i the powerful nation
to the east of Lu's northern border.

Of great interest to Confucius were all three
for they came from families of comparatively low nobility.
Such a course of events came to be
due to a period of relative peace and stability
resultant of a lull in the constant warring for hegemony
in the middle years of the Spring & Autumn Era.
This epoch saw great internal violent struggle within the nobility
as each sought pre-eminence and power
with many a family extinction barely escaping lightly.
In order to alleviate the constant threat of deadly rancour
and enhance the chances of a period of internal tranquility
the noble families opted for neutral parties for the office of Premier.

Men like Tzu Ch'an and Yen Tzu of low nobility
could only have come to prominence under such a condition
to be at the heart of governmental rule and policy formulation
earning commoners' and nobles' support and popularity.
Their fame and influence reached far beyond their borders' restrictions
to the international political arena
Tzu Chan of Cheng and Hsiang Hsu of Sung were remarkable in particular
coming as they were from small impotent nations.

During the twelve State Spring & Autumn Era,
the states aligned themselves to one of the two nations of great power,
Qin and Ch'u heading the northern and southern leagues, respectively.
However, just before the above period in 546 BC
Hsiang Hsu convened an inter-state peace conference
where the two leagues reached peaceful agreement
with relative peace lasting less than 10 years in duration.

The Development of Legalism

Tzu Ch'an made great use of the peace and stability
by generating in Cheng recovery.
Cheng was devastated by constant inroads by the Qin and Ch'u leagues.
However in return for peace Cheng had to pay tribute to both leagues.
To pay this tribute he set in order land divisions and boundaries
and levied property taxes and encouraged economies
in the people's expenditure
And with the surplus that he did gather
he worked and planned for an increase in agricultural productivity.
He had to enforce these reforms by law,
So enacted he such laws
by inscribing them on newly recast bronze vessels,
such as those employed to honour the ancestors at festivals.

Thus the first form of codified law in China came to being.
Hitherto before there was no written law.
And further, within the clan were settled violations of the law.
The clans had absolute authority of their internal running.

Tzu Ch'an's innovation of enforced obedience to a written code -'Legalism',
received from such eminent statesmen as Shu Hsiang of Qin much criticism,
who defended the principle of clan autonomy.
Initially there was much opposition
but after 3 years his policies yielded increased agricultural productivity,
and earlier indignations turned to great admiration.

Development of Rationalism

Tzu Ch'an's political revolution
was matched by his rationalist condemnation
of superstition in the field of reflection,
for states and communities
gathered for the purpose of common religious celebrations.
No distinction was made in such communities
between state and religious functions.

In the time of the Shāng the practice of tortoise shell divination did prosper,
Heaven's will was determined through a study of the cracks that did appear
in the tortoise shell after it was heated.
Such divination the Zhōu also inherited.
It remained an integral part of the national tradition,
To such an extent that at War's declaration,
the choice of general was left to the decision formulated by tortoise divination.

In addition Heaven's Will was found manifest
in celestial phenomena such as solar eclipses and the weather,
in animal manifestations such as birds in flight together,
devastation left in a locust horde's wake
and even a man-made blaze
had the imprint of Heaven's Will manifest

A violent typhoon struck the central plain in 524 BC,
followed by a destructive fire that blazed in four states ferociously,
including Sung and Cheng.
The foregoing year the Master Soothsayer of Cheng
had from astronomical indications predicted a fierce fire
and had urged Tzu Ch'an to give sacrifice to avert the disaster.
Tzu Ch'an refused to countenance such superstitions,
After the great fire the Master of Divinations
foretold of another all consuming fire.
Considerable panic spread through the state,
some suggested that the state capital be located at a less ill-omened place

Tzu Ch'an with the followings words did counter:
'Heaven's way is far removed only man's way is to us near '[22]

---

[22] The way of man, the principle controlling the human world, is near, and can be understood by man; whereas Heaven's way, the will of Heaven is something far removed, and incomprehensible.

Claiming that, since the Master of Divinations
was forever making all manner of predictions,
there were bound to be some occasions,
when his predictions would turn out correctly,
although this was not to be taken as proof of unerring accuracy.

Tzu Ch'an's beliefs sowed the seed of rationalism
a recognition that distinctions between the known
and unknown be made by reason alone.
Ch'an was the first thinker to move away from superstition
towards an age of enlightenment and illumination
Ushering in the separation
of unity of government and religion
Precipitated by a code of written law implying a division of function,
and separation of government and religion.
Confucius was to carry the baton of rationalism.

(Act III) - 527 B.C. Death Of His Mother & The Re-birth of Confucius

On his return Confucius assumed the position of Master of Rituals
at the Temple of the Ancestors'
However, fate which can often be unkind,
his happiness was a fancy most fleeting,
for the proud mother who had seen her son shine
fell ill with fever and soon lay on her bed dying.

(Confucius at his mother's deathbed)

Mother: My darling son, it would appear
Heaven's decree is finally near.
For I, my ancestors calling me hear.

Confucius: But you are still so young mother dear
the fruits of my labour without you would be most bitter.
I still have need of your love and affection.
Lost will I be without you as my foundation!
For without your encouragement, sacrifice and support
I would have amounted to naught.

Mother: A man are you now my dear,
tall and strong just like your father...

Confucius: Wish I could have known him mother.

Mother: Like me he would have been most proud of you my darling.
There are not many like you, morally so upstanding
or who possess a nature so gentle and caring.
Remember to always remain so my darling
and Heaven will grant its favours upon your being.

Confucius: Mother dear I was blessed the day I was born your son,
In kindness and compassion your equal is no-one!
You have but experienced hardship all your life without relief.
And now that I am in a position to provide you relief
you wish me to leave.

Mother: Do not think so Confucius having you was a blessing.
Fortunate have I been to have a child as upright and caring.
I would have liked to have remained by your side a little longer
and seen your successes but my time is now past my dear
I shall always be by your side forever…

Confucius: O mother……..
And as he utters these words…. tears trickle down gently
as a his mother's smile fills his heart with her warmth and love deep,
only for her, to soon after close her eyes gently
as eternal slumber embraces her in peaceful sleep

Confucius: O mother you have left me hollow,
what now is the point of tomorrow!
What is happiness or sorrow?
Without you in my life gone forever
who will now be my confidant, my counsellor?
Who will shower me with such love and affection?
Who about Confucius will now care?
Who my highs and lows will now share?

(With these words Confucius taking his face into his hands begins to weep)

The following morning Confucius informed his friends and family
of the sad news and set about preparing his mother's funeral ceremony.

Though a man humble in terms monetary
Confucius had saved some money
and wanted to give his mother
a burial that all would remember.
Not for any superficial reason
but a sign of his love and devotion
for the woman who though in extremes of poverty
had alone brought him up most devotedly.

Confucius first paid call to the local draper
and bought a yellow silken shroud to drape his mother
and piece of pristine white cloth that he hung from the frame of the front door
and a wind gong he placed to the right of the door.

He bathed his mother's body and with talc it powder.
and in a resplendent white phoenix floral patterned dress he clad her.
In the coffin did he lay her body gently
and with the yellow silken shroud draped her body softly
and placed ornate jade bìs[23] one atop and one under her body.
Then placed did he a ceramic vessel of great beauty
with dragon handles that he had purchased for his mother.

Next four cóngs[24] did he lay
around the cadaver
and the coffin did he place
in his mother's chamber.
Then informed all his relatives and friends of his mother's passing
Throughout the day the mourners kept steadily coming
to their deepest commiserations and prayers offer,
and to donate what little money they could muster.
All were impressed by the way he had presented his mother's body
according to the proper dictates of the ritual ceremony.
The coffin was closed finally
and lifted by his friends and family
and it to the cemetery did they carry
with great dignity worthy of the nobility.

They walked to the outskirts of Qu'fu city,
until they finally came upon a verdant place
with many a tree and dug the grave
and finally lay the coffin down gently.
Confucius covered the coffin with earth till it finally did disappear
and saying his final good byes, home returned a sad and lonely figure.

---

[23] A *bì* (璧) is a flat disc with a hole in the middle

[24] A *cóng* (琮) is a four sided tube with a round hollow centre, often with monster masks carved around the corners

(Confucius Sings whilst playing the se)

O sweetest soul to me most dear
That I had the honour to call my mother
In your love you did me bathe
In your love you refuge me gave
Your gentle honey'd smile
from my disappointments kept me alive
In your sweet words of support
I forever found Hope
Now bereft you have left me
All in this world forever lonely

(And in silence does he weep)

The solemnity and splendour of the burial ceremony
with which he his mother's remains honour,[25]
struck his fellow citizens with wonder
and they determined to bury their dead similarly
with ancient honours in the future.
Soon bar the really poor his example was followed by all in Lu society
and spread to the neighbouring states and further.
Like a loving son mourning for his beloved mother,
Confucius shed many a melancholic tear.
Paying his appearance scant regard
he his fine garments did discard.
After three days he partook of food only to sate his hunger
but when he ate he was not conscious of any flavour.
And when he heard music, he felt no pleasure,
Such was Confucius' grief-stricken nature.

Confucius was unhappy as he was unable to rest his mother
next to her husband as of his father's tomb he had no idea,
and so he enquired around Qu'fu,
until he came upon a woman from Tsou by the name of Man Mu
'In Fang[26] shall you his grave discover',
and finally with her husband did he bury his mother.

[25] An old custom which had fallen into disuse
[26] 9 km east of the capital of Lu

Confucius' Three Year Solitude
& His Moral Compass

So, the reverent Confucius passed three years in mourning
a time he dedicated to philosophical study.
reflecting deeply on the eternal laws of morality,
tracing them to their founding source,
he determined to make it his life's course
to follow the path of righteousness
and enlighten his countrymen in the precepts of goodness,
and inculcate in them a desire for virtuous living.

A few days later we find Confucius in the depth of depression
and lost in deep contemplation…

Confucius: O Confucius, who are you?
What's to become of one such as you
in this world so cruel and depraved,
where a man's worth by the chance of birth swayed?
Though you may of nobility many generations before emanate
but you like many of noble ancestry
were brought up in a humble state.
Is your lot to remain an insignificant personality
wandering the rest of your life with thoughts of impotence you so hate…?

How has it come to be
that we are ruled by corrupt and debauched rulers so carefree
who abuse there position so recklessly with complete impunity,
paying little regard to their citizens' miserable existence,
they tax them to a life of meagre subsistence
treating them like their slaves to do with as they please?
Surely this immoral state of inequity cannot stay unchallenged free?

Where is the moral compass of Kings Wen and Wu?
These Zhōu inheritors can their blood really run so morally untrue!
Have their souls truly become devoid of righteousness?
Of course fool! The nature of humans veers towards selfishness
with little regard to the welfare of their neighbour!
People are selfish by their very nature
and those in wealth and power
are only doing what is natural behaviour!

No that cannot be, humans are not selfish by nature,
though they do what brings them personal gain.
I am sure if they comprehended fully
the effects of their behaviour
they could be persuaded to change.
Education…can surely change their selfish personality.

The people had forgotten their Way and led a life of ignorance
Confucius immersed himself in the study of 'The Odes and Document's
to get for his thoughts some inspiration.
And begin the process of enlightenment
He loved playing the se and singing for spiritual enrichment.

黍離 **Shu Li**[27]

彼黍離離、彼稷之苗。
行邁靡靡、中心搖搖。
知我者、謂我心憂、不知我者、謂我何求。
悠悠蒼天、此何人哉。
彼黍離離、彼稷之穗。
行邁靡靡、中心如醉。
知我者、謂我心憂、不知我者、謂我何求。
悠悠蒼天、此何人哉。
彼黍離離、彼稷之實。
行邁靡靡、中心如噎。
知我者、謂我心憂、不知我者、謂我何求。
悠悠蒼天、此何人哉。

[27] *Shī Jīng* (The ancient Chinese Book of Odes) Song No. 65

The Millet

There was the millet with its drooping heads;
Drooping down the heavenly millet in perfect harmony
did gently sway.
Its motion slowly did make me wonder,
My heart all-agitated .
Those who knew me,
Said, sad was my heart .
Those who did not know me,
Said I was seeking something.
O distant and azure Heaven!
By what man was this [brought about]?

There was the millet with its drooping heads;
Drooping down the heavenly millet in perfect harmony
did gently sway.
Its motion slowly did make me wonder,
My heart intoxicated with grief.
Those who knew me,
Said sad was my heart.
Those who did not know me,
Said I was seeking something .
O thou distant and azure Heaven!
By what man was this [brought about]?

There was the millet with its drooping heads;
Drooping down the heavenly millet in perfect harmony
did gently sway.
Its motion slowly did make me wonder,
For my heart knows everything yet is filled with anxiety
Those who knew me,
Said, sad was my heart .
Those who did not know me,
Said I was seeking something .
O thou distant and azure Heaven!
By what man was this [brought about]?

Confucius: These rulers are corrupt and heartless paying scant regard to *Lǐ*[28]
governing without any thought to the happiness of their citizenry,
whom they regard little more than slaves to serve their pleasure!
Surely the purpose of government is to nurture
one's citizen's happiness and welfare
like the divine and sage rulers and kings of old who did so care?

Kings Cheng T'ang of the Shāng and Wu and Wen of Zhōu Dynasty
were rulers who truly knew their kingly duties
To improve their people's prosperity
rather than enslaving them to their wills' whims and fancies.
Human life is treated so cheap hither,
take the ruler of Wu, who wishing to prevent
bad news he had received from spreading any further
cut with his hands the throats of 7 men who happened to be in his tent.
The divine sages and kings possessed true *Jén*[29]
true Humanity, Goodness, and Benevolence
with great compassion for their fellow men
whilst these rulers and their cohorts revel in spreading suffering and
Malevolence.
True humanity surely requires of a person in establishing himself
tries he to establish others like himself.
And wishing to gain wisdom
helps others also to gain wisdom.

There is a complete lack of *Yì*[30]
in the aristocracy
who can hardly be viewed as being righteous of behaviour
acting as they do in a just and appropriate nature.

---

[28] 禮 Ritual, propriety, etiquette, learning, governance it is basically the interaction with humans, nature, and even material objects. It comprises such diverse subjects as learning, tea drinking, titles, mourning, and governance.

[29] 仁 *Complete virtue* – being 'benevolent', 'Human-ness' the essence of being human

[30] 義 Right conduct, morality, duty to one's neighbour, righteousness – *the moral disposition to do good*

The ruler of one of the small states, of swords had a great collection
and tried out on his subjects his each new acquisition.
Then there was Duke Ling of Chin enjoyed shooting at passers-by
from his tower up high,
for his perverse sense of humour.
Seeing them try to dodge his missiles gave him great pleasure;
when his cook, bears paws to his liking did not prepare
he had him killed in his anger without a care.

Such rulers though maybe uncommon,
but it is not unusual for nobles to their subordinates threaten
who dare advise against their conduct most repugnant
and kill those who continue their protestation.
Hired assassins are used often.
Punishments are so severe and unpleasant.
In *Ch'i mutilation of the feet* is so common
that special footwear is sold in the shops for those who suffer such punishment.

Bribery is pervasive at all levels of society,
from the perversion of justice in favour of individuals
to bribes demanded and received by state ministers
from other state ministers to secure favourable foreign policy.

Adultery and even incest are common practice among the nobility.
Women, even the wives of other nobles are appropriated without ceremony
by those with desire, power and position of authority.

As for *Xin* they are devoid completely
in honesty and probity.
Once the Duke of Lu visited Ch'i,
he was held until he agreed to marry
his second daughter to a minister of Ch'i.
And one ruler of Ch'u, hearing about one of his vassal's wife's beauty,
went there (as he said) to give a feast for this ruler.
Having arrived, he promptly did his vassal slaughter
abolishing his state forever
and carrying off to his harem his wife for his pleasure.

As for *Zhong*,[31] how can there be in this world any loyalty
to the state or for that matter towards other
when aristocrats and states vie constantly with one another
for total hegemony
and are willing to break even the most solemn of covenants,
there motto being: ***If we can gain advantage over our enemies easily,***
then we must advance without any consideration of covenants.[32]

There is a complete breakdown of *Xiào*[33] - love for one's family,
parents, the state and society.
On social relationships is built Society:
Ruler and subject;
husband and wife;
parent and child;
sibling and sibling;
friend and friend.
Society can only truly function
if each person
understands and assumes his/her obligation.

However, these relationships are today
in utter decay.
Let the ruler be a ruler,
the subject a subject.
Let the father be a father
and a son, a son!

There is a complete breakdown of proper authority!
Here in Lu the Dukes for generations,
have been under the Three Huan's rule.[34]
Even the aristocrats have little security,
let alone the plebeians
who suffer at the hand of their nobles most cruel!

Taxed, toiled, expropriated and slain
by the nobles who hold them in utter disdain!

---

[31] 忠 - *'Doing one's best' - putting into practice obligations that one owes to others –*
it is an effort to bring about the well-being of other people

[32] Words uttered by a Chu officer after witnessing the constant breaking of covenants

[33] 孝 - Filial piety

[34] Three families, Meng-sun, Shu-sun and Chi-sun descended from an earlier prince of Lu, Duke Huan whose influence and power had become widespread.

The plebeians dare not rebellion offer
for fear of suffering death by torture.

Travelling noblemen, even outside their dominions
Marauding go - like a plague of locusts,
cutting down trees for fuel,
denuding the fields of their harvest most precious,
damaging the houses in which they lodge,
backing 'requests' for contributions with violence.
During periods of peace are these common.

Frequent wars have brought dramatic suffering.
Forty two years before I day-light did see
the capital of Sung besieged for so long, lay starving
stripped of all their humanity,
the inhabitants were reduced to eating
the flesh of children.
Since they could not contemplate eating
their own children,
they exchanged each others before them slaughtering.

The gradual breakdown of centralized authority
has increased people's difficulty
The number of nobles has increased greatly,
as nobles take on wives many
and with children countless in number
that their names they hardly remember!

Now of noble birth there are so many who rank high
that there are fiefs insufficient, to them satisfy
and fewer yet governmental positions
even for the rulers' near relations,
that they endure a life of penury
equivalent to the common citizenry!
Yet even minor nobility
continue living a life of absolute opulence and luxury
fuelled by taxation of the poor whose lot of abject poverty
they increase daily!

Confucius' Rationalism

Mid-afternoon on a sunny summer's day,
Confucius is sitting in his courtyard shaded under a poplar tree lay,
with a gentle breeze, slowly ruffling his hair, while he his se did play.

Confucius: O what a blissful day…
Bright Empyrean blue sky
with cotton clouds floating by
What a heavenly day

As he plays, his mind is lost to thoughts of Heaven

Confucius: What of Heaven?
People carry out religious duties and obligations
but what of all that if done for superficial intentions.
They make solemn promises and covenants freely
with little respect for their solemnity.
The treaty enforced upon the Cheng state
a few years before I was born is a perfect point in case

Thus did they swear:

If any should fail to do as is enjoined
by this solemn agreement,
may those who preside over men's sincerity
and watch over men's covenants,
(the spirits of) famous mountains and rivers,
the myriad of spirits
and all the deities sacrificed to,
and all our ancestors past
of our seven surnames and the twelve states
may these spirits punish him severely,
that he shall lose his people,
his appointment shall be flung from grace,
his family shall perish,
and his state and clan be utterly crushed.

A fearful oath, yet within two months duration
compelled again was Cheng to transfer
its allegiance under military pressure.
Other states also did suffer
but none with Cheng's regular humiliation.

Such was Cheng's harassment
that at one point it did state
the covenants to be absurd
and asked that it be permitted to swear allegiance,
not to any particular state
but to whichever one acted according to the promised word.

With their actions they debase the worth of such solemn covenants.
Sacrificing animals, and smearing their blood on the agreements' copies.
And the rulers and officers subscribing to the treaties
read them out loud and with the blood their lips they smear.
Along with the sacrifice they bury
a copy of the treaty
so that the spirits might enforce its terms in an appropriate manner
But these covenants are with such regularity discarded
that they are no-longer highly regarded
for none any penalties suffer
that the spirits are supposed to inflict for transgressions of treaties
So the powerful say: *If we can gain an advantage over our enemies,
we must advance without any consideration of covenants.*

If there are no consequences for covenant breaking
then can the spirits really affect the lives of the living?
Do they in fact exist or are they the product of our imagination?
And what is the will of Heaven?
What indeed is its place,
if any in dictating man's fate?

For Might everywhere is right!

In all the states there is constant intrigue
and usurpation of power from rightful heirs and rulers' keep.
Ch'i[35] invades Lu and meddles in its affairs frequently.
they had two heirs to the throne murdered 82 years previously
with the heads of two of the Three Huan's collusion
and set up the son of a secondary wife as Duke under their instruction

[35] Bordering Lu towards it's north eastern border

In Lu the 'Three Huan' do government dominate.
And recently have tightened their hold over power in the state.
When I was 15 amongst the three
they divided most of Lu's revenue and army,
leaving the Duke but a ceremonial figurehead upon them dependent
For what little contributions to him they deemed pertinent

Not happy with even this situation
In 537 B.C. the Chi family
the most avaricious and powerful of the three in position
took over half of the state due to their unassailable military superiority
leaving the other half for the other two families to equally apportion.

Confucius The Educator

(Man's Nature)

One spring's morning
having completed three years of mourning
Confucius resolves to change a society
based on birth and voracity
knowing that good governance only came to be
when there were leaders who about their citizen's well-being cared.
Rather than take from them every little they had.
The only way he could affect the cycle of change
was by educating the young – the future leaders.

Confucius: So how am I to affect change?
Well you could by giving tuition to teenagers
and turn the minds of the next generation
by teaching them the rituals and courtly refinement
in order they may follow the ways of true gentlemen.
I am certain there is many a parent
who wishes to educate their children
To in future better their predicament.

(Confucius visits the house of his friend Wang Yi)

Yi: Confucius, come in my dear friend.
It has been a while since we last did meet
at your dear mother's passing.
How have you been?

Confucius: Well my dear friend
they have been 3 hard years of solitude and reflection deep
Since my beloved mother's parting
Life for quite a while for me did lose its sheen.

(Yi shows Confucius to the Nan[36] room
reserved for him and his close friends
they sit on the beds and start talking)

[36] South

Confucius: How is your family?

Yi: All fine thankfully.
Mother is as active and busy as ever
looking after my younger brothers, who are resolutely naughty.

(He laughs)
And father well you know the life of a soldier -
always at the beck and call of the Chi family.

Confucius: Indeed I do Wang Yi.
For wherever power lies there is always much conspiracy
that none of anxiety can truly be free.

Yi: There have been rumours of a plot against the Three Huan,
as such the three families ever vigilant remain.

Confucius: Plot against the Three Huan?
Well usurpers can never a peaceful existence hope to gain
And will have their punishment one-day!

Yi: My dear friend ever an idealist you remain
true to your nature you stay.

Confucius: My dear Yi what is a Man without Idealistic fervour!
Nothing but an empty shell that draws no emotive aura!
In Lu like the other states most people live in abject poverty,
while their lords engage in a life of luxury
paid for by bleeding dry the most impecunious
with taxation most onerous.

Yi: That is the prerogative of the aristocrats Confucius
we the commoners
have little say in such matters.

Confucius: I know my dear Yi,
but it is so depressing to see.
Our whole society is dying of moral decay.
The rich and poor have lost their way!

Yi: That has long been the way Confucius,
The rich always act in selfish manner
and the poor are no better either.
The poor too would act in like manner
if they possessed power
People are basically bad Confucius!
Rich or poor makes no difference to Man's nature
for He was born a selfish creature!

Confucius: I understand why you say so Yi,
but with your interpretation of man's nature
I beg to disagree
for good is Man's nature
but without cultivation
due to lack education
ignorant Man remains of bounties greater
that mutual co-operation would bring to He
were He to be shown the way to true pleasure…
that comes from a life of selflessness and morality.

Break free would it the shackles of many an Obsession and Desire
and finally understand would He happiness' true nature.
Inspiration He would discover in poetry.
In Rituals, discipline would his profligate heart temper.
From History He would learn about Heaven's decree,
and the Sage Kings' Benevolent and Compassionate nature,
who ruled not for personal gain
but the happiness of their citizenry.
Then finally Man may see goodness' gain
and the heights His heart's manifest glory.

Yi: O Confucius you indeed are a romantic fool
heady with idealistic notions that your heart rule
but Men's nature veers towards self-gain
and this my friend I still maintain,
rich or poor they are ruled by this common aim.

Confucius: I do understand your reservations my friend
But I still contend
education would open Man's eyes
and He would finally from selfish desires rise
and comprehend the rewards of following the true Way.
The happiness and joy that would come His way
simply by working together for each others well-being
all would share a life truly worth living.

Yi: My dear Confucius
I must confess your idealism is quite infectious.

(He smiles)

Confucius: Well Yi…
one in the goodness of Man's nature must have faith,
for only that, us from the beasts does separate.

Yi: Well Confucius as long as there is one such as you, as guide
there is hope for the ignorant one day to grasp the light.

(They both laugh)

Confucius: Well Yi…..I have decided the young to teach
for devoid of mental corruption
their minds are easy to reach.
With the carrot of education to better their station
I am sure I can extol the virtues of the *Jūnzǐ*'s[37] exalted position
and persuade many to follow His direction
and grow up to become a better citizen and sovereign.
Enabling all to increase their station!

Yi: Don't you think it would be better to pursue a role in government?

Confucius: You know me Yi, I am far to candid to be in government
In addition connections have I none
nor do I possess a silver tongue
to such a handicap overcome.
And as obsequious I could never be
the only solution open to me
is from bottom up to change society.

---

[37] 君子 - The ideal gentleman (human)

Yi: Well a challenge certainly takes your pleasure!
And where will you, your band of young impressionables discover?

Confucius: Well, right here!
I was thinking of your siblings younger.

(They laugh)

But seriously Yi should your parents wish your brothers education
and know of any others of a similar disposition
I would be happy to impart my erudition.

Yi: Well they certainly are a little unruly
and could do with some refinement most truly
benefit would they in the basics of rituals, etiquette and archery.
If you could also archery teach
more people would be willing to send their off-spring.
I will, to my father and mother of this speak
and see if they would be willing.

Confucius: Archery…that indeed is an idea most worthy
for young men also need physical training
Thank you Yi…..
Well I must now be leaving
I was thinking of a few other friends visiting
as well as heading into the city
and of my services information disseminating.

Yi: Well not before having dined with me.

Confucius: How could I refuse, your mother's cooking ….
her food is always a prospect most mouth-watering

(So they sit and eat and talk some more)

Thus it was that Confucius the Educator
began his teaching career,
soon sent to Confucius for schooling was many a teenager.
Teach them would he the virtues of a healthy mind and body.
They would practise archery and learn rituals, history, and poetry.
He tried to instil in them the importance of Lǐ
for he believed it to be the source of right action in all behaviour,
living life from a place of respect for the other
was at the heart of following the path of the Jūnzǐ.

Lǐ, however, does not come to one's consciousness naturally.
It has to be cultivated carefully.
One must first learn and then practice the art of being in integrity,
respecting every human's dignity
and then become committed to, and disciplined in, the practice of Lǐ.
Confucius was trying to turn them into young gentlemen
***he would say to them - the Jūnzǐ is fond of* Jén[38] -**

"The Jūnzǐ does not grieve that other people do not his merits recognize.
His only anxiety is lest he should fail to theirs recognize."
He is an unselfish soul who possesses Shu[39]
and is always faithful to all, old and new
friends, family and strangers will find him the same.
Values he *Xin*[40] and you will find him of an honest and trustworthy name
who will always keep to his promises without thought of self-gain.

The Jūnzǐ is fond of Yi[41] and acts in just and appropriate behaviour.
It is important to cultivate a perfect moral state
in order to set a good example to others.
The Jūnzǐ of *Xiào's* importance gathers
love for one's family, parents and state.
Society is built on social relationships of which there are 5 in number

---

[38] Human goodness/virtue
[39] Reciprocity - thinking out what your obligations to others should be: you should use yourself as an analogy when determining what would be beneficial to others. What you perceive as beneficial to yourself you may reasonably conclude would be beneficial to others; what you perceive as harmful to yourself, you may reasonably conclude would harm others.
[40] 信 - integrity
[41] Righteousness

Obedient devotion in the son and Kindness in the father
Gentility in the eldest brother and Humility and Respect in the younger
Obedience in the wife and in the husband towards her Righteous behaviour
Humane consideration in elder and Deference in junior
Loyalty of ministers and subjects and Benevolence in the ruler

If these relationships are respected amongst all harmony
there surely will be.

Confucius was a most kind and benevolent young master
who treated his students with respect due to an elder.
In turn his young students held him in high esteem appreciatively.
Soon his name began to gain fame in the city
and being true to his motto that *'in education,*
there is no class distinction'
he allowed the children of the poor
to attend for a fee of some dried meat and no more.
He never turned away any
who wished to learn earnestly,
for he believed in good education
as a stepping stone towards helping man's moral erudition.
After a few years not only teenagers came for schooling
but also young men in their twenties refinement seeking
wishing to learn the essentials of noble behaviour
in order to further in government their career.

Confucius & The Viscount D'an

At 28 Confucius as an educator was regarded highly.
This same year saw the visit of Viscount D'an[42] to the court of Lu
The Viscount was a man of great learning and nobility
whose knowledge of ancient administrative regulations was matched by few.

(At the banquet hall of Shu-sun Chao-tzu the Premier of Lu)

Shu-sun: Lord D'an I have heard it related
that during the ancient Emperor Shao Hao's reign[43]
He, his officers after birds did name.
Can this account truly be accepted?

Viscount D'an: Well my Lord Shu-sun, it is indeed true
For during Emperor Shao Hao's reign
Male and female phoenices from Heaven to him flew,
on this good omen his officials decided he, after birds to name.
And then did come, the Golden Emperor
who gave cloud names to every officer.
He in turn was followed by the Fire Emperor,
who used terms connected to fire.
And Kung Kung names related to water
and Tao Hao dragon names to every officer.

Shu-sun: Your knowledge of the ancestors is most enlightening
Lord D'an, pray continue and tell us about Shao Hao more.

Viscount D'an: My knowledge is hardly surprising
For Emperor Shao Hao was the ancestor of my state after all

The Viscount proceeded to all Shao Hao's officials name,
thus confounding all present with his knowledge.
Confucius on hearing about Viscount D'an's great knowledge
sought audience with him to learn more about Shao Hao's reign

Confucius arrives at the gate of the Viscount's quarter in Lu
and waits until he is shown through.
Escorted through the courtyard garden
A veritable colourful Eden

---

[42] A vassal of Lu

[43] 少昊 - also known as Jin Tian Shi (2597 – 2513 B.C.)

full of jasmine, roses and many a fruit tree
whose heavenly scent made his head dreamy
and finally to the Bei room where the Viscount resided.
Confucius enters bowing and sees the Viscount already on his bed seated
with retainers on either side for protection needed

Viscount: Please be seated Master Confucius.

(He points to the bed on his left and Confucius sits down)

Confucius: Thank you my lord most gracious.

Viscount: One has come to hear quite a lot about you Master Confucius.

You have amassed quite a reputation as an educator.
They say you great knowledge of the classics possess,
In addition to poetry, music and archery prowess.
Quite the gentleman and scholar!

Confucius: My lord… I am of knowledge but a humble seeker
and search for it wherever.
And at this juncture it has led me to your door.
For renowned are you as great store
of knowledge of the emperors of old.
You are most gracious
to have availed me of your time most precious.

Viscount: Not at all Master Confucius …
It is always a pleasure
a lover of knowledge to discover.

Confucius: Well my lord
at the banquet you happened to impress all
The First Minister and his companions hold you in awe
with your knowledge of the Emperors of old

(The Viscount smiles)

Viscount: Is that so….?

Confucius: Indeed, so.

They say you were able to name quite easily
all the officers of Emperor Shao Hao.[44]

Viscount: Well Master Confucius for me their names come effortlessly
as my father would recount tales of Shao Hao
when I was of age very tender.
Confucius: Would you be kind enough to indulge me a little of their nature?

Viscount: Well Master Confucius, legend does say
the Weaver goddess Huange was his mother
a most sublime and beautiful fairy.
Who whilst drifting on her raft along the Milky Way
Venus, her gaze did discover
falling under his hex deeply.
Shao Hao their union's bliss came to be
A most handsome, intelligent and righteous soul he came to be.
His great uncle, Huángdì,[45]
so impressed was He with He
that named him God of the Western Heavens did He.
Shao Hao in the five mountains of the Eastern Paradise his kingdom created
by birds of all manner and beauty was it inhabited.

As the ruler of this land, He assumed the identity of a vulture.
Of other birds was he the leader,
the Phoenix was his Lord Chancellor,
a Hawk that delegated the law clear,
charged was a Pigeon
of His kingdom's education
and chose He the Four Seasons
to watch over the remaining avian populations.

Although successful for many years was his kingdom,
he moved back west leaving his kingdom of birds to Chong His son.
And with Ru Shou his other son,
He made his home on Changliu Mountain,
where he ruled over the Western Heaven.
In union father and son,
Were responsible for the daily setting of the sun.

---

[44] 少昊 Some say he was the eldest son of The Yellow Emperor (黄帝) and was passed over as emperor

[45] ▪ 帝/黄帝 The Yellow Emperor

Confucius: Of Emperor Shao Hao it is related
fond of music was he
and the twenty-five string lute was by Him invented?

Viscount: Most impressive… for few are aware of His musical creativity!

Confucius: Well my lord of music, a passion I possess
though I must confess
this knowledge I gained from my music master.
Legend apart, from many lips I did hear
that Shao Hao might have been the son of Huángdì
and Léi Zǔ[46] who silk did discover
and was the silk loom's inventor.

Viscount: Indeed Confucius, some say Huángdì
was the leader of Yi.
He shifted the capital to Qu'fu.
And after eighty-four years was succeeded by his nephew Zhuanxu.

Confucius: And what of Huángdì?

Viscount: Well it is said of He,
his conception was signalled by a thunderclap which all could hear.
Huángdì was a vigorous and just soldier-emperor
who fought a fierce battle and defeated Chi You the rival leader.
We owe our writing to him for ordered he his officer Can Ji
to establish Chinese characters and invented the magnet did Huángdì
In addition discover the wheel and the first brick buildings built he.
An observatory to study the stars did he erect,
the calendar did he correct,
and all the land to his subjects was given to redistribution

Confucius: My Lord's depth of learning
is indeed most astounding…..

(The Viscount smiles)

Viscount: A great compliment from a man of such learning….

(And they carry on talking a while longer about the ancient emperors)

---

[46] 嫘祖

(Act IV) - Duke Chao's Pathetic Spectacle & The Conspiracy to Overthrow the Chi Family

At 36 Confucius had become Lu's pre-eminent Educator
as such to him was sent an invitation
to Duke Chao's celebration
honouring Duke Hsian his predecessor.

Dances and music were performed in commemoration
at Duke Hsiang's ancestral temple,
but such was the ducal court's state most ramshackle
due to many decades of decay and privation
that unable was it to maintain
the requisite group of musicians and dancers as custom did ordain.

For custom was it usually
in a formal celebration in honour of the state ancestors,
a performance of dance, with music, with 8 rows of performers,
each row containing 8 members,
thus being 64 in number the dancers.
Present at the ragged dance however were, 2 dancers only.

(Watching this pathetic spectacle Confucius felt ashamed)

Confucius: *O how shameful it is here to be*
in the presence of such poor spectacle to see.
It brings shame upon the state
when it's Lord's fate
dictates a life of penury and dishonour
when he can only but two dancers muster
who can hardly be called in addition,
the most proficient in their vocation.

The following day it came to pass that at the festival
held in the household of the Chi family temple,
In commemoration of their ancestors
There was a performance of dance, with music, with 8 rows of performers,
each row containing 8 members,
thus being 64 in number the dancers.

On seeing such a dazzling spectacle the sole preserve of the Zhōu emperor
Confucius sighs in great indignation at these lords arrière:

The impudence of Chi P'ing-tzu *to out-do his superior!*
Such brazen effrontery!
Whilst the rightful Prince of the state lives in poverty,
they entertain eight rows of dancers in his hall decorated so ornately!
He who does not shame
from this spectacle to refrain,
nothing could ashame!
How sad such bad decorum the Chi without fear deign,

Prince Kung Wei the Duke's son incensed at such presumptuous behaviour on the part of the Chi, seething - into action he goaded his father

Kung Wei: Father, how can you stand by such outlandish effrontery
on the part of these insolent Chi!
Who is the Prince of Lu?
You or Chi P'ing-tzu!
I tell you father, ignored this simply cannot be!
This utter humiliation deserves a riposte military!

Duke Chao: Patience my son, Chi P'ing-tzu's brazenness has not passed me.
For this insult he shall pay dearly!
Not content with usurping all my authority
by making all governmental offices of power
his hereditary discretion
he now also deems fit to seek my public humiliation.
This shall not be like the failed rebellion of 13 years prior,[47]
when the secret plans of that loyal mayor
Nan Kuai of Pi,
to drive out the Chi family
and to the ducal house return their rightful power and authority,
were discovered, before we could, to his aid come swiftly.

Kung Wei: I take it you have a plan?

Duke Chao: A most cunning plan!

(He grins)

I wish you to go and invite Chao-po
head of the Hou clan to my presence tomorrow.

---

[47] 530 B.C.

Kung Wei: Why ever so father?

Duke Chao: Don't question your father's order!

Kung Wei: As you wish father.

Kung Wei does his father's bidding
and Chao-po presents himself to the Duke the following morning.

Chao-po: Your Highness, what a pleasure to you see.
How may I of service to you be?

Duke: Morning Lord Chao-po.
I wish to put to you a mutually beneficial proposition.
The illustrious family Hou
just like my House have suffered great humiliation
by the Chi family for many a generation.
Is that not so?

Chao-po: Undoubtedly so.
They were behind my grandfather's assassination
and on numerous occasions have goaded and belittled our family.

Duke: P'ing-tzu thinks because he has Qin's[48] protection
untouchable he remains to do as he pleases without worry.

I am sure of the latest insult upon the ducal house you must be aware
By openly staging the dance reserved for the Zhōu Emperor.
of humiliating me publicly he does not care.
This brazen usurpation deserves a response proper.
Compared to the Tsang[49] you are no less illustrious a family,
Renowned are you for honour and gallantry.
I say it is time we ended our subservience to the Chi!
I know of other families willing to join us against the Chi.
Together we have sufficient men to take on their military.

What say you to such a proposition!

(Feeling proud of the introduction and comparison)

48 The leader and most powerful state of the Northern League
49 The next most powerful family after the Three Huan in Lu

Chao-po: I say .... enough to humiliation!
It would give me great pleasure
to see His Highness restored to His rightful power.
You need but appoint the hour.....

Duke: Good I knew... I could count on your loyal support.
Once we have rid ourselves of the unsavoury Chi
I promise to you handsomely,
with position and power reward.

Chao-po: His Highness is a most gracious Lord....
This humble servant is most happy to serve his Lord.

(And so Chao-po leaves with a smile of quiet satisfaction)

Kung Wei: I see your plan now father....

Duke: Well my son, now we have the support of the Hou family
we will be able to muster more support will be far easier.
Go and summon Tsang Ch'en the head of the Tsang family.
The Tsang family as you know are a most distinguished clan in Lu,
And though to the Three Huan they are inferior in power,
they enjoy a certain degree of acknowledge prestige in Lu,
having produced many a statesman eminent and wise in nature.
For generations they had been on amicable terms with the Chi,
until P'ing-tzu gave to one of their renegades, Tsang Tseng sanctuary.
If we could get their support then the Chi
will stand no chance against our combined prowess military.

And so Kung Wei does his father's bidding
and the next afternoon Tsang Ch'en presents himself to the Duke's calling

Duke: Welcome Tsang Ch'en, long has it been
since you were at my Court last seen.

Tsang Ch'en: Indeed it has been....
How may I be of service to you sire?

Duke: Well I wish a mutually beneficial proposition to you offer
which I hope you will find agreeable
should you be to it amenable.
It has been long since that renegade Tsang Tseng justice did escape
when refuge P'ing-tzu to him gave

Even though your brother he did murder ruthlessly
over an intrigue with his wife that he had maintained secretly
Tell me, is that not so?

Tsang Ch'en: It is undeniably so.

If I could lay my hands upon him only,
I would cut his pretty head swiftly!

Duke: And though the Tsang and the Chi
had been on terms for many a generation most friendly
P'ing-tzu not caring to hand him back, steadfastly refused
Thus usurping the Tsang's prerogative to judge their accused
He has also caused friction amongst your illustrious clan
By wishing to replace you with Tseng as head of the clan.

Tsang Ch'en: Indeed Highness we have heard of such a notion,
but as long as he has P'ing-tzu's protection
we the Tsang are unable to seek retribution

Duke: Well, my friend as you must now know
that upstart P'ing-tzu continues to humiliate me so!
And with his latest grandiose exhibition
of the dance reserved for the emperor's station.
He has gone too far in his pretension!

Tsang Ch'en: I agree Highness his brazen usurpation
has caused upon all good men great consternation.
What does His Highness propose?

Duke: Well, I have enlisted many an illustrious family's support.
The Hou clan for one are willing to join forces against P'ing-tzu.
Together we will banish the Chi forever from Lu.

Are you willing to fill the ranks of our military?
It would be such a pity
not to have in our ranks the distinguished Tsang.

Tsang Ch'en: Well, if with you are the Hou so are the Tsang!

So while P'ing-tzu was about staging the dance, euphoric
and given to grandiose and extravagant dreams, most princely,
a plot to overthrow in one move his rule, most autocratic
was being hatched in strictest of, secrecy.

So One day in the ninth month of the year 517 B.C.
expeditious it was regarded to storm the stronghold of the Chi
when Shu-sun Chao-tzu, the Premier, was out in the country.
Seizing this opportunity
the disaffected young nobles leagued with the Hou clan
and raised a force which stormed the country seat of the Chi clan
Caught of his guard P'ing-tzu fled to a tower
standing at the battlements corner
which the young noblemen and Hou did besiege
with great satisfaction and glee.

(P'ing-tzu in conference with his retainer Chung Li)

P'ing-tzu: I can hardly believe what my eyes see
that weakling of a Duke how did he,
to attack me possess the gall!
How in Heaven's name did he muster such a force!
Where are my useless cousin allies, the Meng and the Shu?

Chung Li: My Lord, there is many a noble family in Lu
that covet your family's position.
The Hou your neighbours have harboured such ambition
for revenge and to regain their past prominent reputation
and the Tsang you angered by giving Tsang Tseng protection.

P'ing-tzu: That wily Duke, I have underestimated.
Mistake was mine to friendship of many generations with Tsang ended
by offering Tsang Tseng sanctuary.
How will I now escape my folly!
I could offer to the suburbs of the city to retire,
though I doubt, if the Duke and his cohorts sensing victory
be amenable to such an offer.
Well Chung Li.... I can but try and see
Go and inform the Duke my offer.

Chung Li loyally went and informed the Duke of his master's offer
However, the Duke buoyed by being on the cusp of victory
and remembering years of humiliation at the hands of his inferior
was not about to let P'ing-tzu of the hook so easily
and declined the offer.

Duke: Tell your master that nothing bar his complete removal
from Lu would be acceptable!

(Back at Ping-tzu's)

Chung Li: I am afraid the Duke is in no mood for negotiating.
He requests your family's complete removal from the country.

P'ing-tzu: Well it was worth asking.
So the daring Duke believes he cornered has me?

Well inform his Highness (**sarcastically**) that should he allow the Chi to retire
to Pi,
I would, to resign my ministerial post be willing.

However this was also declined

P'ing-tzu: That dog! Well as my loyal allies Meng and Shu
appear to have abandoned me
thcrc is little option but to be exiled from Lu.
Inform his Highness that should he allow the Chi
to load the family wealth on chariots, five in number
we will leave the state without bargaining further.

However, this too was declined

A far-sighted loyal retainer,
by the name of Tzu Chia-tzu
urged the acceptance of such terms by the Duke,
but the Duke only sought the Chi's unconditional surrender.

Tzu Chia-tzu: Your Highness, I beg you to reconsider the offer.
You will be rid of P'ing-tzu and his family forever
should you grant them in defeat a little dignity.

Duke: You do not understand Chia-tzu how he tormented me!
How dare he seek a conditional surrender!
I shall make this upstart pay for his insolent behaviour.

Tzu Chia-tzu: Is that wise sire?
We still have to contend with the Meng and Shu.
Should we request an unconditional offer,
they might not be willing to relinquish power.
Should the Chi with their wealth be exiled from Lu
that might also precipitate their departure.

Duke: Enough Chia-tzu!
With P'ing-tzu's unconditional surrender,
they will before me cower
and happily relinquish all power.
For might is always right Chia-tzu!
Now that I have the upper-hand finally
These usurpers will not go unpunished free!

Realising that the Duke was in no mood to accept P'ing-tzu's offer
Chia-tzu this subject did not broach any further.

Meanwhile, an old retainer of the Shu-sun family
left in command during the absence of his lord's trip to the country,
had gathered the members of his household,
and began to address them so:

Retainer: 'We the retainers' fate is linked to the Shu-sun's prosperity.
We do not presume to know anything
of the interests of the state as a whole.
Should this day we the Chi Lord not support all
tomorrow the Duke will on Shun-sun's gate come knocking!
And then who will be able to resist his military?
Were the Duke to defeat the Chi
he would force the Shu-sun family into exile undoubtedly
and this would affect our livelihoods directly.
I say to you all which for us is better,
that the Lord of Chi live or the Duke him conquer?

'Should perish the Chi Lord,
mark will it also, the end of the Shu-sun Lord!'

All those gathered replied immediately
Unanimous was the decision to send a force of military
to help rescue the Lord of the Chi,
The Meng-sun clan also little time wasted
in adding to the unit of the relieving soldiery.
When with the combined professional forces of two households confronted
the motley units of the army under the Duke were routed thoroughly.
And when Chao-po head of Hou was slain
All resistance to an end came.

Duke Chao fled in exile to the state of Ch'i
until his death seven years later.
This was the first time in Lu's long history
that her Duke was expelled from his realm most dear.
Confucius having seen the proceedings unfold so disastrously
was dismayed with the whole affair
and knowing of P'ing-tzu's high-handed tyranny
found such a prospect unbearable to consider
so decided to follow the Duke into exile in the state of Ch'i.

Confucius: O when will these aristocrats realise that greed
only misfortune in the end does breed.
If only the Duke had accepted the conditional surrender,
he would now be enjoying the prerogatives of his rightful power
instead of suffering humiliation once more at the hands of P'ing-tzu
exiled as he is now from his beloved Lu.
How can I live in a state where the usurper P'ing-tzu
has an even firmer grip on the reins of power in Lu?
To sail away to the land of barbarians, better it would be.
But no, how could I with the barbarians be?
For my mission is to educate
and show the civilized states 'The Way'
Better I follow the Duke to the Ch'i state
and see if the people there would be amenable to what I have to say

(Act V) - Confucius' Self-exile to Ch'i

Thus at 36 Confucius followed his Duke in exile reluctantly.
His beloved Lu was but a small provincial country
While Ch'i's capital on the other hand was arguably
the largest metropolis of the Zhōu dynasty.
Having immense strides in commercial and industrial development made.
And long before, Ch'i impression had made
in her Duke Huan providing,
one of the Northern League's leaders most outstanding,
it had for many a generation
in Lu's affairs been meddling
as well as open military conflict with it engaging.
Confucius the interference of Ch'i notwithstanding,
was excited at setting foot in her capital Lin-tse, finally
for of its sounds, sights and attractions, many a tale heard he
that in him had evoked wonderment and fascination.

And so we find Confucius in Lin-tse's enchantment,
wandering and wondering in amazement
at all the hustle and bustle of the metropolis so busy
It was quite a thing leaving his village to go to Qu'fu to study
but this was on a scale altogether grander
which his mind could not quite untangle clear.

Confucius: *O Confucius, so many people did you ever see*
all teeming about their business busy?

To his right were many stalls
selling all manner of fruit and vegetables,
whilst on the opposite side there were a few butchers
with meat and live poultry.
Next came the spice sellers
with their vivid hues and intoxicating scents, spicy.
Confucius' head and eyes were spinning
as he took in the wonders of his surrounding.
As he walked to the end of the street
to his right he found himself in a street
full of silk drapers
selling the finest silks- a myriad of colours.

Confucius: *Well Confucius, all-consuming has become your thirst and hunger...*
you better a place to drink and eat soon discover
before you lose control of your senses here.
But where to find a place to sate my stomach's desire?

(Confucius asks a passer-by)

Confucius: Excuse me friend, but where may a traveller
to this fair city find a place to sate his hunger?

Passer-by: Well friend, Jing's I have found always to be
a place fair of price and food mmm delicious mouth-wateringly.
Just turn left at the next street and miss it will not your nose,
for the smell of the *mian tiao*[50] will lead you to it close.

Confucius: Most kind of you to come to the aid of this stranger,
for the hunger pangs cannot be delayed any longer.

(They both laugh and part their way)

Confucius: Mmmmm what a delicious smell indeed…

He walks into Jing's place resting his weary feet
and orders a bowl of vegetable mian tiao most mouth-watering indeed

Confucius: A most appetizing bowl
of mian tiao I must say landlord,
the like of which I have not tasted
since my mother parted.

Landlord: Thank you kindly.

Confucius: Tell me good sir, where may one find a place to sleep?

Landlord: Well I do a few rooms keep.

Confucius: That would be wonderful, as I am most weary.

[50] Noodles in soup

The landlord shows Confucius to his chamber
Confucius enters and is most happy
to lay on the straw bed most comfy.
And as soon as his head rests, he is in deepest slumber.

The next morning having breakfasted
Confucius resolves to discover the wonders of the city.
As he walks the streets soon he hears the most mellifluous melody
leading Confucius captivated
to the College of Musicians' door.
Seeing something that he had never experienced before,
an orchestra with many a student the Eight Sounds[51] ***playing***
Confucius under its hex, is lost in his musing

Confucius: *O what Heavenly melody*
do practice the Ch'i!
Such sublime sounds that transport the soul
to heights never experienced before...

And finally when the music ended awoke he from his slumber
Entering he went up to the Music Master

Confucius: Forgive me Master
but I am to your city, a humble traveller
never before have I heard music so enchanting.
Pray tell me what is this music that you were playing?
I never imagined music's beauty
could reach a pitch so heavenly.

Music Master: This enchantment is Shao Music young man
a gift of the Emperor Shun to man.

Confucius: It is of Empyrean origin indeed?
I play the lute and *se* but not like that of your students here.
Would it be possible to be taught by you Master?

Music Master: It would be possible indeed.
It is always a pleasure to teach the soul's nourishment
to those truly seeking Heaven's allurement.

---

[51] (八音) silk, bamboo, wood, stone, metal, clay, gourd and hide instruments

Confucius: That I am Master,
you shall find me a most diligent learner.

And so it was for three months studied he assiduously
under its trance falling
all thoughts of food and sleep forgetting
devoting to his lessons utterly
for what Confucius learnt in Qu'fu
from the pre-eminent Music Master of Lu,
by contrast old-fashioned did appear,
and now naïve to the ear.

Lauded by all was his extreme devotion,
his Master, fellow students and soon all in the city
were talking about his dedication.
Eventually news of Confucius assiduity
even reached the ears of Duke Ching
who wished this earnest learner from Lu to discover
and so summoned Confucius to his court did Duke Ching.
Confucius arrives at the resplendent palace's gate
where the captain of the guards did him expectantly await
to the duke's private chamber
did he Confucius usher

(Confucius enters and bows)

The Duke looks at Confucius and finds himself in awe of this imposing figure
who appeared to have more in common with a soldier

Duke: So you are Confucius of Lu
the man who has intrigued in this city quite a few.
Although, from your appearance I must declare
you appear to have more in common
with my captain
than a man of musical flair.

Confucius: My stature sire I owe to my father
Captain in rank a soldier.

Duke: That certainly explains your frame,
pray tell me what was his name?

Confucius: Hu-Liang Ho of Tsou sire,
was my father.

Duke: Hu Liang, mmm I am sure of that name I am familiar…
Surely not Hu Liang Ho
who distinguished himself so
with his might and valour
at the siege of the forts Pi-yang
and Fang!
Confucius: I believe the very same sire.

Duke: A braver man I have yet to discover.

The siege of Fang I do well remember.
Though we had it surrounded,
your father boldly escorted
under darkness' cover
Lord Tsang-sun Ho his master
through our besieging army's might
and immediately retraced his steps back inside
much to our humiliation.

Confucius: Of my father I have little recollection
as he died when I was an infant, sire.

Duke: Your father was a courageous and mighty officer,
you obviously possess his stature.
But tell me how is the son of such a distinguished soldier
come to offer our music such devotion?

Confucius: Well Highness, music is a divine gift from Heaven.
It is the manna of the soul
that refreshes and nourishes it to its core.

Duke: Well I must say, I have never heard of music in such description,

(He affectionately smiles)

Tell me, are you a man of music or do you follow any other profession?

Confucius: Well sire I have practiced many a profession
but before I came here I did teach the young of Lu
the Way of Kings Wen and Wu.

Duke: Pray enlighten me as to what exactly you mean?

Confucius: Well sire I try to teach to those learners most keen
a love of certain qualities of nobility
prized by Kings Wen and Wu highly,
such as *Xin* – honesty and trustworthiness;
Shù[52] – selflessness and faithfulness
towards all friends, family and strangers;
Lǐ the norms of proper social behavior
as taught by fathers, village elders and government officials;
Yì – the ability to be righteous and act in a just manner;
Jén – practice of benevolence and humanity;
and Xiào – love for one's family, parents and country.

If one develops these in the young, then I believe
society as a whole, shall from such upstanding citizens benefit reap.

Duke: Confucius, you are a most interesting character
and I find your thoughts most compelling in nature.

Confucius: My Lord is most gracious.

Duke: I have not been intrigued by any for a long time Confucius.
Pray what is your opinion
on the secret of good administration?

[52] Reciprocity, altruism, consideration for others etc… *'what you do not want yourself, do not do to others'*

Confucius: Well sire, it consists in the prince
being prince,
the servant
being servant,
father being father
and son
being son.

Duke: Excellent! Indeed when the ruler
is not a ruler,
the minister
is not a minister,
the father
not a father,
the son
not a son,
although I may have all the grain I need,
shall I ever get, to it eat?

And pray what is the duty proper
of the ruler?

Confucius: For that sire,
One need only to Heaven's Mandate consider:
to rule Justly Fairly and Wisely
in the interests of the citizenry.

513 B.C. State of Qin leader of the Northern League codifies law inscribed on bronzes

(Confucius in discussion with Duke Ching over Qin's codification of law and on the superiority of Virtue over Legalism)

Duke: Qin it would appear
have Tzu Ch'an's way finally followed
inscribing their laws, making me wonder
whether we in Ch'i should their example have followed.
After all Cheng from it, has great economic benefit gotten.

Confucius: Sad a day sire, for the Duke Wen's Ways are being forgotten.
These laws have been inscribed to fill the coffers of Qin's military
than for any economic gain for its citizenry.

Duke: But surely it is a necessity
To have a strong military
and the only way to finance it is through written regulations
that are clear beyond whims and disputations.
Moreover, inscribed law provides the best solution
to bring within the legal system the whole population,
for in the present system of the law of clan
many who are outside the clan
go unpunished for their transgressions,
as any punishment of transgressions
is at the clans' sole discretion
only they can decide any clan disputation.

Confucius: Yes, but if you use laws to direct the population,
and punishments to control their action,
the laws they will merely try and evade,
and doing so will feel no shame.
But if by virtue you educate and guide them,
and by ritual you control them,
there will be a sense of shame,
and doing right they will not evade.

Duke: So you believe in educating the plebeians
in *Lǐ* the norms of proper social behavior
and *Yì* the ability to be righteous and act in a just manner
and by *Jén* you wish to instil humane and benevolent behaviour?
But can these qualities be truly taught,
surely the nature of Man veers toward many a '*wayward*' thought
for Man is moved by profit and beauty
and has a susceptibility to hate and jealousy,
all of which, if indulged, lead to disorder and criminality.
As such laws need to be proscribed surely?
And followed with threats of punishment for any transgressions!

Confucius: Sire men by nature are very similar,
only by practice come to differ.
Only the wisest and the stupid are not given to change.
I believe most from wrong-doing would refrain
were they afforded an education
that would promote self-cultivation.

Through the practice of ritual one can develop a man's good nature.
Show him *Dào* the ideal Way of life – of virtues and sincerity,
Teach him respectfulness,
justice, and kindness
paying full attention to *Lǐ*
Let him practice music and he will realise its superiority
for unlike law it neither derives authority from governing bodies
nor is it open to the vagaries of the governing bodies.
Dào is independent, for from itself does it derive its authority.
It is a uniformed standard that can be applied to all and sundry
whether they be in Lu, Qin or Ch'i.

Duke: And who is to set this moral guide
and engender love in them for *Dào*'s light?

Confucius: That sire is the ruler's moral obligation.
He has to ensure his government educates the population
by personal rule and moral behaviour
and this implies the ruler
choosing state officials
who are upright and judicious.

(The Duke smiles)

Duke: Morally upright rulers and officials
now that would be a task indeed to such people discover.
Tell me Confucius would you be interested in educating my Prince heir?
He certainly could do with some refinement of character.

Confucius: It would be an honour sire.

(At The Prince's chamber)

Confucius: Tell me my lord what in your opinion
is the most important trait in a person?

Prince: Without doubt strength and power,
if a person has these then he need not defer to any other.

Confucius: That as maybe,
but there will always be someone more powerful and stronger.

Prince: That as maybe,
but I would much rather be in a position of strength and power.

Confucius: And from where does power and strength arise?

Prince: Training one's body leads to physical might
and noble birth dictates power.

Confucius: And in your opinion how best can a noble retain his power?

Prince: By ensuring all minions,
fear his wrath and anger greatly.
A lord should punish any dissent or criticism severely.
Resolute of mind he must be,
without resorting to advisors he must make decisions.

Confucius: Fear….that is indeed a mighty weapon,
but have you ever considered *Jén*
the ability to be humane and benevolent
and *Yì* – to be righteous and just to others in manner,
These foster love and loyalty that is far stronger
then fealty through fear and punishment.

Heaven's Mandate 'To rule justly fairly and wisely
in the interests of the citizenry

Prince: I disagree *Yì* and *Jén* are signs of weakness!
People only respect strength and firmness!

Confucius: That is not strength but weakness, surely,
for people who follow a lord through fear
can be bought or frightened easily
by someone with greater power,
whilst Love people follow unquestioningly
for Love nothing do they fear.

Prince: That is pure idealistic fantasy,
and not appropriate to reality.

And so they carry on in this vain a while longer
with the Prince unmoved by Confucius' persuasive power.

As Confucius becomes at the Duke's court a regular
and has the Duke's ear
much to the courtiers and the Prince's anger.
The Prince resents being taught by a person of birth lowly
how to correct his lifestyle in accordance with morality
a concept which he deems beneath his birth Princely,
as such he and the courtiers conspire against Confucius.

Oblivious to the conspiracies against him, Confucius
who was so enamoured by the whole façade of the urban metropolis
that had moved his spirit initially
now began slowly to question his unreserved admiration of Ch'i
as he finally awoke from Ch'i's captivation
by its florid civilization
and came to the conclusion……

Confucius: 'Ch'i, by one change, could to Lu's standard reach:
Lu, by a single alteration, would the Way reach.
This florid civilization that is the Ch'i
is not altogether different from my unpretentious Lu.
I have too hastily rejected the culture of Lu
and adopting that of Ch'i.

Both the Duke of Zhōu's Way could follow easily,
though Ch'i, has undergone great change and modernization,
but with a slight rectification,
it would to Lu identical be,
whilst Lu with a small amendment
would be restored to the Way most excellent.

Confucius gradually turns back towards a greater appreciation and re-estimation of the worth of the culture of his native Lu. As he learns from his Music Master Ch'i's situation realises that things were to all intents and purposes the same as in Lu.

(We find the two at Jing's sharing their evening repast)

Music Master: I must say Confucius
the taste of food here is most delicious
as is the fragrant wonderful…
And this bowl of mian tiao is truly delightful

Confucius: I have always found the bowl of mian tiao
most satisfying…

Music Master: Well I must say to my stomach it is most pleasing
especially with some bai jiu.[53]

Confucius: Quite so…

(They smile)

Music Master: Gan Bei![54]

Confucius: Gan Bei!

(They down their shot of bai jiu)

Tell me Master of the political situation
in your nation?

---

[53] White rice wine with extremely high alcohol content
[54] Bottoms up!

Music Master: Well Confucius thirteen years prior in Ch'i[55]
the most influential families of this country,
happened to be three - the Ch'ing, T'ien and Ts'ui.
At first the most influential were the Ts'ui,
but angered by his wife and the Duke's illicit liaison,
the family head of Ts'ui to murder the Duke was driven.

Ts'ui family however, was soon made to suffer
for the T'ien and the Ch'ing
supported for the vacant throne Ts'ui's choice Duke Ching,
in return the Ministries of the Left and Right they did insist,
as such the two controlled the government arbitrarily.
But, soon between the Ts'ui and the Ch'in there was a rift
the Ch'ing attacked swiftly
and the Ts'ui completely massacre.

Confucius: Usurpers, always greed and power hunger,
and in bloodshed their fate, they in the end discover.

Music Master: Indeed.. Gan Bei!

Confucius: Gan Bei!

Music Master: Gains of blood and lust last long never.

When the Ch'ing took sole control over the office of Premier
they to a life of utter debauchery did surrender,
spending their time drinking and hunting
and all manner of licentious and immoral behaving.
This soon led to internal disorders,
which was a propitious sign for the other nobles.
Led by the T'ien they their forces united
and the Ch'ing they defeated
who to the state of Wu were obliged to flee
seeking sanctuary.

---

[55] 548 B.C.

The Head of the T'ien being of cautious disposition
did not wish to vaunt their influential position
but schemed to work in harmony
with the old noble Houses of Ch'i,
and secured the advancement of a popular
and able administrator in Yen Tzu as Premier,
however, the real power lay with the T'ien Leader.
Thus we suffer the savage despotism of the T'ien family in Ch'i.
And what of your native country?

Confucius: Well Master sadly the situation is most similar
We also have three families who have usurped the duke's power
and have been pulling the reins of power for many a year.
And as you must be aware our duke now resides exiled in Ch'i
as he failed in his attempt to wrestle power from the Three.

Music Master: We live in times of trouble and intrigue unfortunately..
where peace is an elusive commodity.

Well enough of such matters of sorrow
Lets play a song to lighten our minds my dear fellow.
Do you know *Guan Ju*[56]

Confucius: Indeed I do…

[56] ▪ 睢 - is part of the first section of the *Shī Jīng* entitled "Zhou nan" (周南), itself a part of "Airs of the States" (國風) and has been dated to the seventh century B.C.

(They both sing and play together)

▪ 雎

▪ ▪ 雎鸠，在河之洲。
窈窕淑女，君子好逑。
参差荇菜，左右流之。
窈窕淑女，寤寐求之。
求之不得，寤寐思服。
悠哉悠哉，辗转反侧。
参差荇菜，左右采之。
窈窕淑女，琴瑟友之。
参差荇菜，左右芼之。
窈窕淑女，钟鼓乐之。

Guan-guan the osprey cry,
Upon the islet in the river.
The beautiful, virtuous young lady,
A fine mate for our prince would be.

Varied in length is the duckweed,
Borne left and right by the flow of the river.
The beautiful, virtuous young lady,
Waking and sleeping, he sought her.
Sought her but found her not did he,
Waking and sleeping he thought about her.
Yearn did he her longingly;
Tossing and turning all night long for her.

Varied in length is the duckweed,
Left and right we gather it.
The beautiful, virtuous young lady,
With lutes and zithers, let us bid her a welcome friendly .
Varied in length is the duckweed,
Left and right, we harvest it.
The beautiful, virtuous young lady,
With bells and drums let us our delight show, in the lady.

(Act VI) - Return of The Master 510 B.C.

Sorrowful and disillusioned by what he saw in Ch'i,
Confucius resolves to return to his native country.
And so it was in the year 510 B.C.,
on the death of Duke Zhao in Ch'i
Confucius returned quite happily

509 B.C. With the accession of Duke Ding
Duke Zhao's younger brother
saw an end to the long term of interregnum in Lu.
On his return to Lu
Confucius began many a learner to gather
attracted by his scholastic and moral thinking.

Through his foreign travels Confucius experience did accumulate
which had broadened his field of vision,
helping him arrive in his life at a position
where he was able to formulate
individual and independent philosophy,
confident in his knowledge and abilities, truly
Confucius to teach the righteous Way was finally ready!

Ten years previously
A member of the Three Huan, Meng His-tzu
on his death to the elder of the family,
had left an injunction
that his sons Meng I-tzu and Nan-kung Ching-shu
should in ritual take from Confucius instruction.

He welcomed all who in the Way sought instruction
irrespective of wealth or birth of the individual.
He never refused to give anyone instruction
even the poor individual
who only a bundle of dried flesh could afford
as payment for the education that he eagerly sought.

Confucius did never
his teachings force upon any learner,
for him the student had first in education
to demonstrate a veritable desire .
Confucius would hint at a solution
and expect his students to figure
the remaining details of the answer
by his own mental erudition.
Thus Confucius' approach to education
was in essence
'developmental' in the literal sense.
Of his educational methods he made it clear:

'If a student is not eager,
I do not begin to open up the subject for him:
if he is not eager,
I do not help him.
When I have disclosed one part of a topic,
if he does not come back to me enthusiastic
having himself worked out the other three,
I do not trouble again, to him see.'

Confucius' method of instruction
from his predecessors differed greatly
who having committed to memory
some knowledge of ancient traditions
as laid in the Odes and the Documents,
tried simply to them inculcate without critical reflection.

Thus Confucius' new method attracted many new admirers
and 77 learners collectively called the Seventy
More than half were from Lu
whilst from other states comparatively few.
Only three of his students came from the nobility,
Nan-kung and Ching-shu,
and one later from Sung named Ssu-ma Niu.
However, most were from the rising class of knights.
The object of many of these knights
was to use their education
in order to secure a position
in service of the country
or of some noble family
Thus Confucius began to attract many new followers

The Early Disciples

Tzu-lu[57]

One Summer's day while sitting under a poplar tree's shade
contemplating at his favourite place
in the woods by the Zhuhui River
His thoughts were interrupted suddenly
by an imposing looking soldier in his full attire
who came upon Confucius unexpectedly

Tzu-lu: A beautiful place to clear one's thoughts don't you agree.

Confucius: Tis indeed……

Tzu-lu: Sometimes it is good to escape life's disappointments
and seek in nature serenity and respite.

Confucius: Yes sometimes it is good to seek a little respite
and put in perspective life notwithstanding its disappointments…
Too often perspective is lost in the mind's confusion…

Tzu-lu: Troubles often cloud reason.
Tell me friend in what do you find the greatest satisfaction?

Confucius: Learning moves my spirit deeply.
And what of your satisfaction?

Tzu-lu: My long sword most decidedly….
the weapon of a knight most trustworthy.

Confucius: True, but what if to your present ability
there were added the results of learning,
then you would be a very superior man surely?

Tzu-lu: Of what advantage to me would be learning?
A bamboo on the southern hill you will see,
which is straight itself without being crooked.
If you cut it down and use it,
you can send it through a rhinoceros's hide easily
what is the use of learning?

---

[57] Also known as Zhong Yu and Ji Lu

Confucius: Yes, but if you feather it
and with steel point it,
penetrate will it not more deeply?[58]

(Tzu-lu bows twice, and says)

Tzu-lu: A knowledgeable Master you are truly..
from you instructions I would receive gladly.

(Thus it was, Tzu-lu Confucius' most trusted disciple, friends came to be)

One day when Confucius was instructing his son Kong Li
there was a knock on the door
Kong Li went to answer
and two young souls did he usher
Min Sun[59] a gentle heart to the core
and Jan Yung a man once imprisoned wrongly.

Min Sun: Master, forgive this intrusion
I am Min Sun and this, my friend Jan Yung.
We have come to seek from you an education,
should you be kind enough to offer us instruction.

Confucius: My door is always open
Min Sun and Jan Yung
to those who seek an education.
All that I require in return
is that the learners apply themselves fully
to their studies to the best of their ability.

Min Sun: I promise sir to apply myself most assiduously.

Jan Yung: That Master will also be true of me,
although I must confess once was I a prisoner
which I hope will not prejudice my entry.

Confucius: Of that have no fear,
for if you come to me seeking learning earnestly
then of my students I ask no more.

---

[58]That's to say an arrow flies straight not only because of the shaft of the arrow, one also needs to add the arrowhead and the feather at the end to make it fly straight. Likewise talented people also need education to make them better

[59] Also known as Tzu Ch'ien

And you Min Sun fame of your filial piety is known to all.
It's not often that one in your position
would have so forgivingly saved a cruel stepmother
from home and family's expulsion
when of your mistreatment your father did discover.

Min Sun: Well sir, it would have been unfair and improper
upon my half-brothers to have lost the love of their mother
had she been made to pay for her behaviour.

Confucius: My dear child, filial piety
is the foundation stone of good government and society.
It never happens that those having cultivated the virtues of filial piety
and submission to elders
will be fond of creating disorder or opposing their superiors.

The *Jūnzǐ*,[60] with the root alone does bother;
and if the root is planted firmly,
the Way grows assuredly.
Filial piety and fraternal duty
are the roots of humaneness indubitably

[60] The Ideal (Virtuous) Human

On Music

(We find Confucius and his disciples Tzu Lu, Min Sun and Jan Yung practising archery in the woods)

Confucius: Well Tzu-lu …lets see how straight your arrow
is compared to your tongue

(He smiles)

Tzu-lu: Well Master I am not sure about my tongue…
but true is always my arrow

What shall our target be?

Confucius: Mmm how about the left branch of that ginkgo tree?

Min Sun: Upon you I would have made greater impression
had it been a musical contest?

Tzu-lu: Musical contest!
Music should not be a real man's occupation!

Confucius: I see Tzu-lu regards music as an unmanly activity
I'd best give up playing *se* instantly.
Or otherwise our good friend for a lady might mistake me

Tzu-lu: Erm ….Given your frame of that have no fear.

(They all laugh)

I did not mean it quite that way Master…
I just see no gain from such a recreation.

Confucius: You should not so be hasty in your estimation.
For education should start with poetry
emphasize *Yi*
and on music reach its completion
For just as archery is good for developing one's physical condition,
likewise music is the soul's nourishment!

Jan Yung: Well Master, though I play no instrument,
music does have the most soothing effect on my soul……

Min Sun: When I play, freed is my soul
from the shackles of mortal reality
to roam amongst the Empyrean clouds free.

Tzu-lu: Well never having picked any musical instrument,
I am unable to your feelings comprehend

I'd rather spend my time aiming my arrows straight and true…..
Confucius: Well let your arrow fly then Tzu-lu…..

(Tzu-lu loads his arrow…bends his bow and aims true and strikes the branch)

A true strike indeed Tzu-lu!
If only to your studies you were as diligent
as you are to your archery
your mind would open to the wonderment
of the true Way and its resplendent glory.

***(As he says so….he lets his arrow fly straight …
striking the branch, landing right next to Tzu-lu's)***

Tzu-lu: A son of a knight you are truly!

**(And as Min Sun loads his bow and lets his arrow soar just missing the branch
four young men Jan Po-niu,[61] Jan Chi'iu[62] and Kung-His Hua approach)**

Jan Po-niu: Forgive our interruption Master,
but I Jan Po-niu and my friends come seeking your instruction.

Kung-His Hua: Indeed, we hope to benefit from your wisdom Master
and make ourselves cultured gentleman.

Jan Chi'iu: An honour it would be to receive instruction
from such an illustrious Master.

Confucius: Well with such silver-tongues,
what need have you of my instruction?

[61] Also known as Jan Keng
[62] Also known as Tzu You and Jan You

Jan Chi'iu: Of no use are silver-tongues
if lacking in culture, depth and sophistication
we are of humble stock
wishing to gain knowledge and to better our lot.

(Confucius smiles)

Confucius: Just as long as you remember -
I do not enlighten those who to learn are not eager,
nor arouse those who to give an explanation are not worried.
If having one corner of the square presented
they cannot come back to me
with the other three,
I, to go over the points again shall not bother.

Jan Po-niu : We are here to learn Master
and shall apply ourselves to our studies
to the best of our abilities.

Jan Chi'iu /Kung-His Hua Jan Po-niu: Most assiduously.

Confucius: Then listen to what I have to say carefully

The case for me is like that of someone raising a mound.
If he stops working,
the fact that it perhaps only needed one basketful of earth
makes no difference; I will not move to help him.
Whereas even if he has not got beyond levelling the ground,
but is still working,
the fact that he has only tilted one basketful of earth
makes no difference; I will go to help him.

But as you have promised your best
I can hardly refuse such eager minds request.

So Jan Chi'iu, how are you at archery….
as accomplished as your tongue undoubtedly?

Jan Po-niu: You are most perceptive Master
Jan Chi'iu is quite a shot indeed,
but alas as for me…
I have never the bow been able to master.

(The five laugh and practice the noon away)

On Study & Learning

(We find Tzu-lu, Min Sun, Jan Po-niu,* Jan Chi'iu, *Kung-Hsi Hua with Confucius at his home discussing Study and Learning)

Confucius: Listen to me well *O Young Gentlemen*
Learning is like building an embankment:
If I stop carrying the buckets of earth, it is my stopping.
If, after dumping one bucket-full,
I continue to bring more buckets full,
it is my continuing.

Be inspired by poetry,
guided by the rules of propriety,
completed by music and surely
you will stay on the path of morality.

Remember those who are born wise are the best.
Those who study and learn easily are next best;
those who study but have difficulty learning come next;
and those who are ignorant but do not even study
are the lowest sort of humanity.

The ancient scholars studied for their own improvement.
Modern scholars study in order to obtain others' opprobrium
A scholar who is concerned with comfort and luxury
is not a true scholar most worthy.
And if a man doesn't continually question
What is this?
What is that?
I cannot help in his instruction.

Do you heard of the six defeats that a man from the true Way, keep?

Tzu-lu: They sir, onto us are a mystery….

Jan Chi'iu /Min Sun/ Kung-Hsi Hua: Truly….

Confucius: Then sit and listen to what I speak.
One who loves virtue but does not study is defeated by a lack of direction.
One who loves wisdom but does not study is defeated by ignorance.
One who loves sincerity but does not study is defeated by deception.
One who loves boldness but does not study is defeated by a lack of temperance.

One who loves honesty but does not study is defeated by crudity.
One who loves persistence but does not study is defeated by his own rigidity.
From the age of fifteen my Will was set on learning,
And I can say without boasting
that there are very few men who of learning have such a liking.

Further a love of wisdom, without the love of study,
only leads to superficial generality.
A man who learns without thinking
is enmeshed completely.
A man who thinks but has no learning
is in a state of uncertainty.
Therefore, hear much, and reject what is doubtful….
See much and exclude what is questionable.

Min Sun: I take it Master, *Learning* is not merely memorization
of ancient tradition without discrimination
but consists of the elimination
of the ambiguous from ancient tradition,
and the selection of what is accurate and good?

Confucius: Quite so, it is not mere memorization
Of ancient tradition without discrimination
Zhōu had the advantage of looking back on the Xià
and Shāng culture
and has achieved a magnificent culture.
Though we do not follow
the Zhōu?
Without reflection
there can be no clarification.
Likewise mere reflection on one's own
leaves one in a state of confusion
Knowledge only truly comes with the combining of study and reflection.

Kung Hsi Hua: Master of learning you speak with such passion.

Confucius: To learn quietly my dear children,
without being sated gives me great satisfaction.
Even when merely with two other people I go walking,
I can always learn from their bearing,
for I imitate their good qualities
and avoid their bad qualities.

And to teach others without flagging
such activities are for me not troubling.
However, to study and be presented with the occasion
to put what one has learnt into action
Surely there is nothing that gives deeper satisfaction?

Tzu-lu: It is indeed most gratifying.
And what say you of putting into practice as soon as hearing?

Confucius: I say… why have such a hasty disposition?
Before you act you should consult with your father
and your older brother
And benefit from their discussion.

Min Sun: Mmmm True… a little reflection
can often save a man from ill-thought action

Confucius: Quite so my dear Min Sun
Many a man has come to rue his hurried action

(Later on, Jan Chi'iu asks the same question)

Jan Chi'iu: What say you Master of putting into practice one's study?

Confucius: You should act immediately.
Many a man has come to lament
his delayed intent.

Jan Chi'iu: I see….
Guess many fail to seize the opportunity
that might present itself only momentarily.

Confucius: Quite so
my perspicacious fellow.

(After Jan Chi'iu had departed Kung Hsi Hua asks)

Kung Hsi Hua: When Tzu-lu asked you, you advised him to delay.
When Jan Yu asked, you told him to act without delay.
May I ask why
the difference in reply?

Confucius: Jan tends to give up easily, so I push him.
Tzu-lu tends to leap before he looks, so I restrain him.

On Lǐ (禮)[63] & *Yì* (義)[64]

(Confucius teaching at his school)

Jan Chi'iu: May I venture to ask why you hold *Lǐ* of such importance?

Confucius: In this day and age of decadence
only in the performance of religious ceremony
is there still to be found consistently,
a type of conduct regulated
by a norm of behaviour that is socially accepted
in which men's actions are motivated by pattern of cooperative actions
rather than swayed by greed and momentary passions.

Thus it is the foundation stone of behaving in socially accepted norms,
free from any motivation of greed and passions.
If men learn *Lǐ*
then they will be amenable to the path of virtue undoubtedly.
The forms of ritual practice of *Lǐ*,
are of value, only
if they are the outer and visible sign
of an inward grace, fine.

I cannot bear to see forms of *Lǐ*
by one whose heart no reverence possesses,
For a man who no virtuous behaviour arouses
has nothing to do with *Lǐ*!

It is more important in mourning for the dead
that there be sincere grief, instead
that every rite be fulfilled meticulously.
They say: It is *Lǐ*! It is *Lǐ*!

Does *Lǐ* mean nothing more than a silk and jade display?
In *Lǐ*, rather than being too lavish in display
it is better to err on the side of moderation.

Jan Chi'iu: So can one state
it is akin to good taste -
doing what is suitable in every situation?

---

[63] Ritual
[64] Righteousness/Propriety – doing what is ethically best given a context

Confucius: A most apt description!

Jan Chi'iu: If so, does this mean any practice can change through the times
provided it stands the test of being judged fit for a given situation,
even though it may not have been among the practices of the kings of olden
times?

Confucius: Indeed! The hemp thread cap is prescribed by *Lǐ*
when taking part in rituals which are sacrificial
but nowadays people wear silk which is more economical
and I follow the common practice though it may appear contrary to *Lǐ*.

Tzu-lu: So I take it *Lǐ* is more than just for ceremony.
It is a kind of balance of conduct
preventing excess or deficiency,
guiding towards the middle road of socially beneficial conduct.
Lǐ thus distinguishes the civilized man from the rude barbarians
who give immediate and undisciplined vent to their emotions?

Confucius: Absolutely!
Courtesy, if not regulated by *Lǐ,* becomes laboured pompousness;
Caution if not regulated by *Lǐ*, becomes mere timidness;
Courage if not regulated by *Lǐ*, becomes mere unruliness;
Frankness if not regulated by *Lǐ*, becomes mere effrontery.

Jan Po-niu: But surely *Lǐ* is nothing more than polished form of polite
intercourse between gentlemen and courtly dandies -
nothing more than superficial courtly ceremonies,
punctilious in manner but lacking in any personal force.

Confucius: *Lǐ* if it were mere civility,
as opposed to expressing good character, is not *lǐ*.
The *Jūnzi*[65] understands *Yì*.
The *Xiǎo Rén*[66] understands *Lì*.
Right is the basic substance of the gentleman's character;
He carries it out by means of *Lǐ*.

---

[65] The ideal human being often translated as a *gentleman* or *superior man*. The *Jūnzi* literally means 'lord's son' (the ruler's son). Despite its literal meaning, for Confucius any righteous man willing to improve himself can become a *Jūnzi*

[66] The *petty (selfish) man*, who does not grasp the value of virtue and is more interested in self-gain

If in a man's natural qualities he is uncultivated;
if his training exceeds his natural qualities
he is little more than a lackey who is educated.
It is only when the natural qualities
and the training complement each other harmoniously
that we have the gentleman proper.

Min Sun: I take it then *Lǐ* is a means of disciplining the emotions
and establishing a balance in one's actions –
preventing excess and parsimonious nature?

Jan Yung: Whilst, *Yì* represents what is ethically right and proper
in a given situation
and the *Jūnzǐ,* by observing the rite
and because of his virtuous inclination
always knows what is right.

Confucius: Indeed! A man who in literature studies extensively,
and who disciplines his learning with *Lǐ*,
will not overstep the bounds lightly.
However, a true gentleman performs *Lǐ*
not because of any selfish reason but for the sake of *Yì*,
for he understands it to be right intrinsically.

Min-Sun: In that case the foundation of *Lǐ*
rests upon *Yì*
for while pursuing one's self-interest is not bad *per se*
one would be a better, more righteous soul
if one's life followed a Way
designed to enhance the greater good of all,
an outcome of *Yì*.
This then is doing the right thing for the right reason presumably?

Confucius: Precisely!
A most perspicacious lot you are certainly.

(**He smiles gently**)

***As time passes by more and more students to Confucius gather
as he gains a reputation for being a virtuous educator
and soon attracts the attentions of new Duke Ding
and the Chi K'ang Tzu
who was to become the de facto ruler in the year 492.
And so in 508 B.C. Confucius is invited to the palace of Duke Ding***

Duke: Ah Master Confucius…so kind of you to entertain me.
Hopefully you will be able to impart some of your wisdom on to me.

Confucius: You are too kind sire,
However, I am but of knowledge a lover
That is all
and no more.

Do I regard myself as a possessor of wisdom?
Far from it? But if even a simple peasant comes in all sincerity
To ask a question of me,
I am to thrash out the matter ready,
with all its pros and cons openly,
to the very conclusion

Duke Ding: Tell me Master Confucius
know you of a single sentence
which could make a nation prosperous.

Confucius: Such an effect cannot be expected from one sentence.
However, there are some who the following do believe:
To be a prince is the contrary of easy;
to be a minister is certainly not easy.
If a ruler understands this truly
the difficulty of his princely duty
may there not be expected the prosperity
of his country from this one sentence?

Duke: I see, and is there a single sentence
which can ruin a country?

Confucius: Such an effect as that cannot be expected from one sentence.
However, there are some who say this—
In being prince I have no pleasure,
but only in that no one any opposition can offer
to what I utter!
If a ruler's words be virtuous in nature,
is it not also good that no one oppose them?
But if they are not good, and no one opposes them,
may there not be expected the ruin of his country
from this one sentence ?

Duke: Indeed! Everything does from above filter
if that is corrupt
then everything that is under
shall with that disease too become corrupt.

Tell me, how should a prince
employ his ministers
and how should ministers
serve their prince?
Confucius: A prince should employ his ministers
according to the rules of propriety;
and towards their prince the ministers
should offer their fealty freely.
When a prince's personal conduct is correct,
his government is effective without the issuing of orders.
If his personal conduct is not correct,
he may issue orders but they will fall on deaf ears.

Lead the people with governmental measures
and regulate them with laws and actions punitory,
and they will avoid wrongdoing
but will have no sense of honour and shame.

Lead them with virtuous examples
and regulate them with rules of propriety
and they will avoid wrongdoing
through a sense of right and shame

(Act VII) - 505 B.C. Confucius The Revolutionary

The 7 years when Chi family was under P'ing-tzu
marked the apex of the Three Huan's power.
Ironically this period also sowed the seeds of their fall too
the Chi family had delegated to their retainers power,
Drawn from the new class of knights they eventually revolted
And with the death of P'ing-tzu it was all precipitated

We find Chi Huan-tzu
the elder son of P'ing-tzu
with friends and dancing ladies enjoying
their indulgent evening
interrupted by Yang Hu the Head retainer of the Chi family
who whispers in Chi Huan-tzu's ear grave news

Yang Hu: My lord it pains me greatly
to be the bearer of grave news
I am afraid to say Lord P'ing-tzu
breathed his life's end but a short while ago suddenly.

(Chi Huan-tzu calms himself)

Huan-tzu: Thank you Yang Hu,
Alas death visits all eventually.
Please be kind enough to inform the rest of the Household
And ask them to come to me.

Yang Hu: Yes of course My Lord
Your orders shall be carried out swiftly.

(And as Yang Hu leaves, Huan-tzu stands up makes his excuses and leaves)

Huan-tzu: I am afraid my dear friends
I have been informed politely
of a certain husbandly duty
that I had promised this night to my sweet lady.
But pray continue your night of revelry
as I must take leave of you my dear friends.

(They all laugh and so Huan-tzu takes his leave)

In Huan-tzu's private quarters we find gathered Yang Hu
some senior retainers and the whole Chi family.

Yang Hu proposes that the precious state jewel of Lu,
which he had worn as his tenure of regency,
to be enterred with him for his after-life's journey.

Yang Hu: Sir it would be quite proper
were Lord P'ing-tzu be buried with full distinction
and as such it is my opinion
that we bury him with the state jewel to him honour .

However, Chung-liang Huai a loyal steward of the Chi
in whose care the jewel came to be
refused such an action steadfastly

Chung-liang Huai: Sir, I strongly disagree
this jewel is a sign of authority
and heritage as such it should pass to his successor you
and your successors in turn too.

Huan-tzu: My dear Yang Hu
I understand your desire to honour
most highly Lord P'ing-tzu,
but on this occasion
I must side with Chung-liang's opinion.

Yang Hu: Sir, I humbly beg to disagree,
For Lord P'ing-tzu
made supreme the House of Chi in Lu
and as such he should be honoured accordingly.

Huang-tzu:[67] I agree with Yang Hu,
this family owes a great deal to uncle P'ing-tzu.
We have never before achieved such prosperity
dominance and power as under your father
and as such it is only befitting and proper
that such a great man we bury
with this precious treasure
as a mark of our reverence in his honour.

---

[67] A cousin of Chi Huan-tzu

Kung-fu Wen-po:[68] I am with Huan-tzu.
Though our uncle was a great man and made Chi
the supreme power in Lu
and should be honoured appropriately.

The gem however, is no ordinary jewel
but a symbol of our power and rule
as such it should remain visible to all and sundry
of the Chi's wealth and supremacy.

Yang Hu: This is outrageous sir, I cannot believe your selfish nature,
I must say I am most disappointed with your manner
I expected a lot more from the son of P'ing-tzu!

Kang-fu Wen-po: How dare you speak to me so Yang Hu!

Yang Hu: I dare because none of you are worthy to succeed Lord P'ing-tzu
GUARDS! Seize all these members of Chi so unworthy.
Drag them to the open square in front of the southern gate of the city,
for all to see their nature so niggardly.

And so all the clan members are dragged to the southern gate of the city
Where the people quite bemused look upon the proceedings nervously

Yang Hu: All you gathered and members of Chi,
I hereby request you take an oath agreeing openly
to Kung-fu Wen-po and his supporters' expulsion
with only Huan-tzu's exception
as they have defiled the late Lord P'ing-tzu's memory
with their nature so selfish and miserly!

Having no choice but death they all readily did agree.
Having succeeded in bending the will of the Chi,
Yang Hu, began to amass all power in Lu,
By sidelining the new Chi Lord Huan-tzu

Thus the tables were turned on the Three Huan's supremacy
for their oligarchic rule
gave way to the despotism of the upstart Yang Hu the Cruel,
who held the reigns of power in Lu for years three.

---

[68] The most popular member of the clan against the burial of the jewels

He won over the disaffected
of the Chi and Shu-sun clans,
together with their servants and retainers,
and put to death the chief members
of the Three Huan clans
for whom he felt any personal aversion
and to bring them all over to his faction
he busily plotted.

After three years of despotic de facto power
Yang Hu sets about hatching plans to cement his rule further
We find him with his cousin Yang Yueh mulling things over

Yang Hu: I've got rid of all the Three Huan's leading members
bar Huan-tzu, who I shall deal with in due course
but the problem is how to persuade without force
the other noble families' members
to ally with me

Yang Yueh: Hmmm.. That cousin is a problem that needs addressing urgently.
The noble families to follow are unwilling
someone, who from noble birth does not spring
unless ...that is......

Yang Hu: Unless that is....?

Yang Yueh: Tell me Yang Hu,
who is the most respected individual in Lu.

Yang Hu: Mmm...well none amongst the Three Huan are worthy
and that puppet Duke Ding could hardly arouse respect worthy of fealty.

Yang Yueh: Exactly...so who is left, who commands respect most
praiseworthy?

Yang Hu: Well there is only one whom all revere and respect...Confucius?

Yang Yueh: Exactly all in Lu laud the virtuous nature of Confucius!

Yang Hu: You sly dog ...you wish me to offer him a governmental position
and so in return, give my rule some claim to legitimization.

I know he has sought public office but he is a man of high morality
he would never to such a proposition agree.
He will see through my intent easily.

Yang Yueh: Well cousin, that I shall leave to you to figure,
for when you wish to,
you can be quite persuasive in nature....
just imagine though if he were to ......

Yang Hu: That indeed would be the perfect solution.
Go this instant and to Confucius extend my invitation!

(Yang Yeuh arrives and finds Confucius' in the company of Tzu-lu at the stables)

Confucius: What do you make of this stallion?

Tzu-lu: It certainly is a steed strong and handsome..

(Yang Yeuh approaches)

Yang Yueh: Greetings Master Confucius, pray forgive this intrusion,
but I have been sent by Lord Yang Hu
who next Friday will hold a banquet for the distinguished gentry of Lu
and naturally to the most brilliant son of Lu
extends he his warmest invitation..

Confucius: Yang Hu is far too kind in my adulation,
for I am but a humble teacher imparting a little instruction.
I am afraid I must respectfully decline his invitation
as prior engagements have me at a distraction.

Yang Yueh: Surely Master Confucius, a day's postponement
would not be out of the question?

Confucius: I am afraid even a solitary day's postponement
would simply be out of the question,
I pride myself in keeping to each and every obligation
and these engagements require my particular attention.

Yang Yueh: Well Master Confucius that is indeed a pity,
Yang Hu was looking forward to the pleasure of your company.

Confucius: I am afraid it is simply,
an impossibility.

Yang Yueh realizing that Confucius could not be persuaded reluctantly leaves defeated

Yang Yueh: It would appear I will have to disappoint Lord Yang Hu.

(Taking his leave he rides back)

Tzu-lu: That scoundrel Yang Hu,
I wonder what motive drove him to you?

Confucius: Quite simple Tzu-lu,
he wishes I presume for me to accept some office in his government.

Tzu-lu: Why ever would he think he could persuade you
one of such high principles to his government?

Confucius: For that reason exactly!
He believes by persuading me to join would give his rule integrity.

Tzu-lu: That upstart usurper!

Confucius: Maybe so Tzu-lu but most clever.

(Yang Yueh back at Yang Hu's house)

Yang Yueh: I am afraid that old fox to deceive is not easy
and did decline your invitation.

Yang Hu: Well it was too much to expect that on the first occasion
he would accept my invitation so readily.
Well I do not give up that easily.
I shall have sent to him an offering…
a pig as a sign of my respect saying:
that Yang Hu had sorely missed his company
and hopes that he will have the pleasure
of his distinguished personage in the not too distant future.

Yang Hu thereupon sent Confucius his offering,
Confucius seeing through the motive that was underlying
waited for an opportunity
when he knew Yang Hu could not home possibly be
to pay his visit of gratitude personally.
However, the two met on the street accidentally.

Yang Hu: Come! I wish to speak with you.
Could it be called an act of 'humanity'
to possess a valuable jewel such as you do,
and cheat your state of it's benefits so callously ?[69]

Confucius: No, it certainly cannot be.

Yang Hu: And can one who in spite of a desire to serve his country,
forever fails to grasp opportunity after opportunity…
really be called wise?[70]

Confucius: I must profess such conduct cannot be defined wise.

Yang Hu: Time is slipping,
and the years for us keep on rolling.
Accept in my government a position
and at long last put your theories into action,

Confucius: Very well I will your offer
duly consider.

In the end, against his original intentions,
he was unable to resist Yang Hu's importunity,
and consented to serve him finally
However events would confirm his reservations.

Yang Hu summons the Head of the Chi, Huan-tzu,
with the pretext of offering sacrifice to the founder of Lu.
The real intent was to murder Huan-tzu

---

[69] Meaning that one who possessed the genius of Confucius, could not be styled loyal to the community if he refused to serve it: such refusal would engender misgivings on the part of the populace, and could not be termed 'humanity'
[70] A hint at Confucius' trip abroad to Ch'i, and his inability to turn the times to advantage in his various attempts to influence political matters.

in the courtyard where the sacrifice was to be,
and to this end, Yang Hu had, a day previously,
issued a proclamation
for all war-chariots in Qufu's mobilization

Suspecting something unsavoury,
the Head of the Meng-sun family
had advised his colleagues to be
on their guard constantly

but on the day in question,
Yang Hu sent Yang Yueh his trusted cousin
To 'escort' Huan-tzu
from his seat in the country to Qu'fu.

Yang Yueh: Your carriage awaits.

Huan-tzu: It most certainly waits…..

Huan-tzu with great reluctance steps on the carriage,
driven by the personal coachman to the Yang family
and they drive towards the ceremony
with Yang Yueh in the the following carriage

(During the drive)

Huan-tzu: Tell me I surely know you?

Lin Ch'u: Indeed you do Lord Huan-tzu
for I am Lin Ch'u
Once a guard to your late father Lord P'ing-tzu

(He sighs)

Huan-tzu: I never forget a face my dear Lin Ch'u.

Your voice appears filled with sadness and nostalgia?

Lin Ch'u: My Lord is perceptive like his father
Your father was a most generous and great Leader

A man certainly…
worthy of loyalty…

Huan-tzu: He was a great loss to the family
And now we have arrived at this state, so sorry...

Lin Ch'u: It gives me no pleasure
t see your family arrive at this sad juncture

Huan-tzu: My dear Lin Ch'u
It is still not too late for you
to fulfil your loyalty
to the Chi family.

Yang Hu's hold on power is but temporary.
We the Chi are not helpless completely.
Drive me to the house of the Meng family
and I promise to reward your loyalty
most handsomely.

Lin Ch'u: Well My Lord Huan-tzu,
having eaten from the hand of Lord P'ing-tzu
it is only correct that I repay his generosity
Now with my loyalty to the Chi.

***Lin Ch'u, swerves from the road suddenly
and to makes off in the direction of the Meng family
Yang Yueh and his escort did them pursue
But they were unable to prevent Lin Ch'u
from reaching the Meng family.
Yang Yeuh is killed instantly
and a violent street battle does ensue
between warriors loyal to the Meng family,
and the troops of Yang Hu
The battle was decided when a large force of military
arrived from the base fort of the Meng family.***

***Hearing of the defeat Yang Hu
made his way into the palace of the Duke of Lu,
stripped off his armour,
and donned civilian attire.***

***He the palace vaults did raid,
And a precious jewel and large ceremonial bow take,
all hereditary treasures of the state.***

And after spending one night nervously
in the suburbs of the city,
the following day across the border did he flee,
to the state of Ch'i.

(Confucius commenting on the affairs to his students thus spoke)

Confucius: When the Way prevails in the world,
ritual, music, and punitive expeditions will proceed
from Emperors' hands.

When the Way prevails not in the world,
ritual, music, and punitive expeditions will proceed
from princes' hands.

When such things proceed from princes,
there will be few who do not lose power
within ten generations.

When they proceed from the Senior Officers of princes,
there will be few who do not lose power
within five generations.

When they proceed from the retainers
of Senior Officers
many will lose their hegemony
within three generations indisputably.

When the Way prevails in the world,
government will not be
in the hands of any Senior Official.

When the Way prevails in the world,
there will not be
any call for discussion among the people.

Confucius thus highlights the transfer of power
from the Zhōu especially during the Ch'un-ch'iu era
with the decay of the Royal Way of the Zhōu Dynasty,
there came a gradual transfer of administrative authority
to persons of status lowly.
With the fall of Yang Hu,
Kung-Shan Fu-Jao who governed the Chi stronghold of Bi

did not immediately leave Lu
but held the city of Bi in revolt against the Chi,
wishing under his protection
to restore power and position
to the Duke of Lu.
He like Yang Hu
Also sends to Confucius an invitation
to accept a government position.
(Confucius unravels the message in the presence of Tzu-lu)

Tzu-lu: Who is the message from Master?

Confucius: From Kung-Shan at Bi

Tzu-lu: And what business does that scoundrel have with you Master?

Confucius: Well he summons me to join him at Bi.

Tzu-lu: Such presumption!
Surely he must know of your opinion
that you would never entertain such a proposition?

Confucius: Well Tzu-lu, I am mightily tempted.
Maybe with my assistance change can be initiated
to rid Lu finally….
of the rule of despotic nobility.

(Tzu-lu displeased)

Tzu-lu: I implore you do not go!

Confucius: O Tzu-lu why must I not go?

How can it be that he summons me
for a purpose that is improper?

Tzu-lu: Was it not you who once taught me
it was wrong to use force against one's superior?

How can it be
that you wish to go to the side of a usurper…
for surely
he used force against his superiors
the Chi - his employers.

(Confucius gives up the idea of joining Kung-Shan and says)

Confucius: O Tzu-lu, maybe,
but certainly he did not for nothing call me.
If there is one who will use me,

here in the East I could make for him a Zhōu!
Right and wrong are not always easy to discern my good fellow.
Surely the Chi
have dominated government for generations forcibly
usurping the ducal house's authority?

Tzu-lu: A usurper is a usurper!
Though, be bad his master
he should not turn against or abandon
the hand that fed his self.
For otherwise a morally wicked person
is he himself.
Not a person in whose company
You should be.

On Poetry & Dào[71]

After the disappointment of the rebellion's failure
Confucius, became a disillusioned character,
However, solace he found anew
with the arrival of two bright stars new
Yen Hui and Tzu Kung
whilst extolling to his son, Tzu-lu, Min Sun and Jan Yung
the importance of poetry
as being the embellishment of one's study

Confucius: My children why do you not study Poetry?
Were you to study it assiduously
it would stimulate many an emotion,
your sympathies broaden,
help you be more observant…
moderate of injustices your resentment.
It is useful at home in one's father's service,
and abroad in one's prince's service.
Further, it will amplify
your familiarity
with names of birds, beasts
and trees.
If you do not study Poetry
you will be
like a man standing with his face to a wall
which for an educated soul will not do at all.

(Confucius talk is interrupted
by the arrival of two young men in their early 20's,
Confucius beckons them to come)

Confucius: Come my children…enter

(They move towards him hesitantly)

Yen Hui: My name is Yen Hui Master.

Tzu-Kung: And I am Tzu-Kung Master.

Confucius: And what brings you young men here?

---

[71] 道

Tzu-Kung: My friend and I wish ourselves in education to further.
And there is no man wiser
or any teacher greater
to learn from, than you Master.

Confucius: Well of flattery
you certainly seem to have a mastery.

(He smiles)

Yen Hui: We wish to be students of the Way,
should you be so gracious
as to us teach Master Confucius
though I am ashamed to say
coming from an impoverished family
I am only able to pay
some dried meat as tuition fee.

Confucius: As for payment never fear
I accept any who ten pieces of preserved meat can offer.
All that, I in return of my students seek
is that they are earnest in their study.

Your sentiments, in one so young are promising
For if a man hear the Way in the morning,
he may die without regret in the evening.
However, remember those who merely know it
are not equal to those who love it;
and those who love it
are not equal to those who delight in it.

Now hear you all carefully
a gentleman, in making his plans, thinks of the Way;
he does not think of making a living.
Even if one tills the soil with hard labour,
he may on occasion suffer hunger;
and if one studies, he may be able to earn a better living.
The gentleman's concern is about the progress of the Way;
he does not worry about poverty.

And you Yen Hui
what do you understand of the Way?

Yen Hui: Dào…is the ideal way of life
for the individual and the state.
to emulate
It is a way of life
which includes all the virtues, sincerity,
respectfulness, justice, kindness, and the like.
It pays full attention to the rules of propriety
and to music alike.

However, like the human body,
it is more than the sum of its parts;
when followed in its entirety
it suddenly starts
to attain a character
and power that to it, is peculiar.

(All including Confucius are amazed at the depth of this young man's understanding)

Confucius: Bravo…. a most lucid description.
Dào is also superior to any law or regulation
as it stands the test of time itself.
While Law is dependent on the vagaries of governing bodies
and derives its authority from those bodies.
Whilst Dao, derives its authority from itself

for it is completely independent
of any government,

Dào is also Law's superior
for it expects more than a minimum standard of behaviour
Dào not only prohibits one from killing
or injuring a neighbour,
but also requires adopting towards one's neighbour
a friendly and helpful bearing.
Dào does not operate by the use of sanctions.

Jan Yung: But if it does not have any sanctions
how can one persuade people to follow Dào,
for the nature of individuals veers from altruistic Dào
towards self-interest.

Confucius: Its stimulus to good is not based on an appeal to self-interest,
because it does not encourage any person
towards virtuous action
by the promise of reward or sanction,
it does not turn the individual's attention
back on himself
on what is profitable or unprofitable for himself.
This is important because if the individual comes to the conclusion
that his own interest and profit are ultimate end of action,
he will do what is morally right only so long as the advantages
outweigh the disadvantages.

However, if the individual strives to follow Dào,
the self and its interests cease to be the focus of attention.
For his standard of action
becomes compliance to Dào
rather than profit for himself.
At the same time, his actions cease to differ
Dào from profit for oneself
as they become unified together
one and the same
through focussing on Dào the common aim.

And now back to our earlier topic… Poetry.
I was just telling my company
of its importance…
perhaps you might have an idea as to its significance.

(Pointing at Tzu-Kung)

Tzu-Kung: Well Master may I venture to say
its importance arises from its use to convey
meaning by allegory
at the disposal of the diplomats' armoury
in their official speeches at conferences
and banquets where they plead their cases
by making veiled references
quoting subtle allusions contained in verses.

Confucius: Bravo! A most impressive summary!
For if you do not study Poetry
you will have nothing to use when called to speak.
Moreover, though a man be able to repeat
all 300 pieces of Poetry,[72]
but if he carries out his office ineffectively,
for example when sent on a diplomatic mission
although extensive be his education
if he cannot make replies without prompting.
Of what use then is his learning?
For this reason intimate knowledge of poetry is essential
to one who would rise to become a high official.

[72] *Shī Jīng* - simplified Chinese: 诗经; traditional Chinese: 詩經

Failure of the Revolution
502 B.C.

After all the upheaval and absolutism of the Chi
followed by Yang Hu's usurpation of authority,
the most important task was the reconstitution
of order of both government and society
which had suffered disruption.
It was imperative to eradicate finally
the errors of the policies
adopted hitherto by the Three Huan families,
and formulate a new overall plan and vision
of benefit for the entire nation.

Within the Three Huan there was not a single visionary
with the talents necessary
to introduce a programme of such enormity
In these circumstances the image of Confucius rose highly
in the minds of many.

(Confucius at the palace of Chi K'ang Tzu)

Worried about the great number of thieves in the nation
Kang-tzu sought Confucius' opinion

Chi K'ang-tzu: Master Confucius…pray come sit beside me.
Kind of you to indulge me finally with your company[73]
I have heard much about your knowledge and wisdom
My cousins like most in Lu hold you in high estimation
and thought maybe
you might impart some upon me.

Confucius: You and your cousins are too kind sir,
for I am of knowledge but a great lover.
Do I regard myself as a man most wisely?
Far from it! But if even a simple peasant comes in all sincerity
and asks of me a question,
I am, to thrash out the matter ready,
with all its pros and cons, to its conclusion.

---

[73] Although he did not become the head of the Chi family until 492 his relationship with Confucius began 6 years prior. It is recorded that he sent a present of medicine to Confucius, who commented, 'Not knowing what it is I dare not taste it.'

Kang-tzu: You are most modest Master Confucius….
I am greatly worried about the number of thieves in Lu.
Perchance you can offer some advice, judicious?

Confucius: Sir if you,
had no improper desires,
they wouldn't steal if you paid them to.

Kang-tzu: Mmmm Interesting but, desires…
Those I have many…..
guess I shall have to curb some… but, …slowly

(He smiles fondly)

Tell me Master Confucius how can one best regulate
the business of the state?

Confucius: To govern is to rectify.
If you lead the people by being yourself rectified,
who will dare not be rectified?

K'ang-tzu: I guess I had better myself rectify
For otherwise nobody will
my orders obey.

(He smiles)

And what do you say to killing unprincipled people
for the sake of principled people?

Confucius: Sir, in carrying on your rule
why should you be so cruel?
Let your evinced desires be for what is good,
and the people will be good.
The character of a ruler is like the wind
and that of the subjects, is like grass.
In whatever direction blows the wind,
must bend the grass.

K'ang-tzu: How can one make one's nation
to reverence their ruler,
to be faithful to him without coercion,
and to go on to nerve themselves to virtuous behaviour?

Confucius: Let him preside over them with gravity;
then they will reverence him.
Let him be final and to all show generosity;
then they will be faithful to him.
Let him advance the worthy
and to the incompetent, teach;
then they will virtue eagerly seek

K'ang-tzu: Quite an onerous undertaking
maybe I can employ some of your disciples
to aid me in virtuous example-setting?
I have heard good things about the abilities of your learners
but I wish to enquire about some from you personally.

Confucius: Well sir, most of my students are of great ability
and assiduous in their study.

K'ang-tzu: Tell me, is Tzu-lu the right sort of person
to put into office?

Confucius: Tzu is efficient - a man of decision.
he decidedly is capable of holding office.

K'ang-tzu: And is Tzu-kung the right sort of person
to put into office?

Confucius: He can turn his merits to account – he is a man of acumen
he without doubt is capable of holding office.

K'ang-tzu: And Jan Ch'iu would he be the right sort of person
to put into office?

Confucius: He is versatile and melliloquent
It goes without saying he is capable of holding office.

Following this conversation
K'ang-tzu took the three into his employment
During these tumultuous times of great instability
K'ang-tzu, knew it was very hard to secure loyalty
and as Confucius was a man of great principles
he knew so too would be his disciples.
On his return, on fire was one of Confucius' stables
and there was great commotion.

Kong Li: Father…father
I am afraid the stables one of the stables is on fire.

Confucius: Did anyone harm suffer?

(Most anxious)

Kong Li: Only one of the horses in the flames suffer.

(Relieved)
Confucius: Poor creature…
thank Heavens no-one else harm suffer.
Horses I can replace but friends never.

(Act VIII) - Confucius' First Official Position

When Confucius was 50 years of age
The Duke offered him his first official position,
Being made the town of Chung-tu's magistrate
which carried with it the supervision
of a number of junior officials.
Under his leadership the city did prosper
and all those …peasants and nobles
who came upon Confucius seeking justice proper
he never did turn away or harry
and found him an impartial arbiter of integrity.

Confucius was no mere provincial politician
with his horizon bounded by the limits of his own nation;
instead with his rich international knowledge and experience,
he towered above many a contemporary
as man a true statesman and visionary,
as such in 499 B.C. he rose to greater prominence,
becoming a Minister of State in an advisory capacity
in the government of his beloved country[74]

---

[74] However, this position turned out to be honorary as on important matter he was side-lined

Part I - *Jūnzǐ (君子)*[75] *Xiǎorén (小人)*[76] & *Jén (仁)*[77]

(Confucius at his home discussing the Jūnzǐ with his disciples)

Yen Hui: Tell us Master how would you define *Jén*?

Confucius: To subdue one's self and return to propriety is *Jén*.
If a man can for one day subdue himself and return to propriety,
all under heaven will ascribe perfect virtue to he.

The man of perfect virtue is cautious and slow in his speaking.
When a man feels the difficulty of doing,
can he be other than cautious and slow in speaking?

Ssu Ma Niu:[78] Are you saying virtue is mere hesitation in speaking?

Confucius: Virtue is so difficult to achieve;
how can you not be hesitant when of it you speak?

Tzu-kung: People say Yung is a man of *Jén*,
but he is not an effective speaker.

Confucius: I don't know whether Yung is a man of *Jén*,
but I don't see why he should be an effective speaker.
Smooth talk breeds hostility.

Tzu-kung: But surely eloquence is an essential quality
when it comes to defeating one's opponents in argument?

Confucius: The *Jūnzǐ* speaks of things that are significant,
but those who are loquacious
are not necessarily virtuous.
Thus a *Jūnzǐ* is courageous
but bravery alone is not the same as being virtuous.

---

[75] The ideal virtuous human being
[76] The petty man (the selfish man)
[77] Perfect virtue
[78] A nobleman from Sung who had become Confucius' disciple

Thus I implore you stay far from clever talkers,
for they are dangerous.
I hate to see sharp speakers
overturning states and clans with their tongues insidious.
They constantly seek advantage
rather than think of acts virtuous.
And he who constantly seeks for small advantage
never achieves things that are wondrous.

Yen Hui: The purpose of eloquence… I take
is not to find the truth but to win the debate,
and to this end the debater will try and evade
as far as possible true reason
and issues of importance?

Confucius: Indeed! Debate and eloquence
are not designed to make an informed decision,
but to people persuade
by appealing to their base
prejudicial emotional state,
by making clever utilization
of humorous turns of expression
rather than profound analysis and reflection.

Tzu-kung: What do you say of a person
who is liked by each and every of his fellow citizen?

Confucius: That is insufficient to judge a person.

Tzu-kung: Then what about a person
who is disliked by each and every of his fellow citizen?

Confucius: That is still not enough to judge a person.
It is far better that he was liked by the righteous
and disliked by the villainous.

Ssu-ma Niu: Sir, tell us, something of the *Jūnzǐ*?

Confucius: The *Jūnzǐ* is free from extremities
is one who follows the middle course,
Virtue's true source!
He goes neither far nor falls short, in his duties
for he is neither impetuous
nor over-cautious.
He has neither anxiety nor fear.

Ssu-ma: So being without anxiety or fear
constitutes being *Jūnzǐ*?

Confucius: Indeed! When internal examination
nothing wrong does discover
why be consumed by apprehension?
What is there to fear?

Ssu-ma: Master my mind is laden with anxiety
and apprehension pursues me relentlessly

for other men have brothers,
only I have no brothers.[79]

Confucius: My dear Ssu-ma if you never fail reverentially
to your conduct order, and are respectful to others
and observant of propriety,
then all within the four seas will be your brothers.

Why should you then be distressed because you have no brother?

Ssu-ma: So true Master….
since coming to you I am no-longer a lonely figure,
many a friend have I, who is worthy of being called brother.

Pray continue Master
about the *Jūnzǐ's* traits most fine?

Confucius: The *Jūnzǐ* has traits nine
which occupy his mind

---

[79] He did have an elder brother Huan T'ui who was an evil sort and Ssu Ma did not wish to call brother

of thoughtful consideration greatly.
In regard to the use of his eyes, he is anxious to see clearly.
In regard to the use of his ears, he is anxious to hear distinctly.
In regard to his countenance, he is anxious that it should be gentle.
In regard to his demeanour, he is anxious that it should be respectful.
In regard to his speech, he is anxious that it should be truthful.
In regard to doing business, he is anxious that it should be reverently careful.
In regard to what he doubts about, he is anxious to others question.
When cross he thinks of difficulties, he may encounter due to this emotion.
When he sees gain to be got, he thinks first of righteous action.

Tzu-kung: Has the *Jūnzǐ* his hatreds?

Confucius: He has his hatreds.
He hates those who proclaim the evil of others.
He hates the man who, being in a low station, slanders his superiors.
He hates those who have valour merely,
and are unobservant of propriety.
He hates those who are forward and unwavering
whilst at the same time, are of contracted understanding.

Yen Hui: How can we increase virtue, overcome evil, and avoid delusion?

Confucius: A most excellent question!
If you place responsibility
over success and victory,
won't your virtue increase?
If you work on your own evil
rather than criticizing others evil,
won't you, your evil defeat?
If, out of a fit of anger,
you your life as well as of your parents' endanger,
isn't that a case of delusion?

Yen Hui: This indeed is the path to righteousness…
people spend far too much on others' imperfections
and lauding their own uprightness
whilst denying their mistakes and transgressions.

Part II - *The Jūnzǐ The Xiǎorén & Jén*

Tzu-kung: And is one able to distinguish the *Jūnzǐ* and the *Xiǎorén*?

Confucius: One is indeed able to distinguish the *Jūnzǐ* from the *Xiǎorén*
as Night from Day can be differed easily.
The *Jūnzǐ* stands in awe of things, three:
the Mandate of Heaven;
great men;
and the words of the wise.
The *Xiǎorén* does not know the Mandate of Heaven;
takes lightly great men;
and laughs at the words of the wise.

Further…..

The Jūnzǐ is not divisive but all embracing.
The Xiǎorén is divisive and not all-embracing.

The *Jūnzǐ virtue* loves;
whilst the *Xiǎorén* material possessions loves.
The *Jūnzǐ* justice and fairness seeks;
the *Xiǎorén* personal favours seeks.
The *Jūnzǐ* sees the strengths and not weakness of others.
The *Xiǎorén* only finds weaknesses of others.
The *Jūnzǐ* lives in harmony with others, but does not follow the hordes.
The *Xiǎorén* is a conformist, and yet with everyone is at odds.
The *Jūnzǐ principle* understands.
The *Xiǎorén* only profit comprehends.
The *Jūnzǐ* remains steady in times of crisis.
The *Xiǎorén* crumbles at the first sign of crisis.
The *Jūnzǐ* exudes self-confidence
but is not arrogant.
The *Xiǎorén* is arrogant
and lacks self-confidence.

Yen Hui: So the *Xiǎorén* is superficial
and fickle?

Confucius: You may say that of his nature.

Tzu-kung: A shallow man lacking any conviction
or direction
apart from self-interest which is his altar?

Confucius: Indeed! Unlike the *Jūnzǐ,*
for whom *Jén*
is of paramount importance
the *Xiǎo Rén* revels in his self-significance.
Tell me, if a man have in him no *Jén*,
what has he to do with ritual, music or virtue?

Yen Hui: *Jén* then is the supreme virtue
and the fundamental principle?

Confucius: Yes, but both virtue, music and ritual
should be a manifestation of *Jén*.

Tzu-kung: Dào's founding principle is then *Jén*?

Confucius: Quite so…the *Jūnzǐ* does not seek wealth and admiration
is not oppressed by poverty and a mean station.
He does not desert *Jén*
even for the space of a single repast;
in moments of urgency,
in times of jeopardy
he remains in *Jén* steadfast;
for if the *Jūnzǐ* were to desert *Jén*,
he would on no account fulfil the demands of his station.

Tzu-kung: So the *Jūnzǐ*'s life is inextricably linked to *Jén*'s realization.

Confucius: Exactly! …. The *Jūnzǐ*
studies literature,
practices ritual, and never for an instant departs from *Jén*.
He always strives to attain to the realization of *Jén*.

Yen Hui: The *Jūnzǐ* then is not one who has achieved it to perfection?

Confucius: Yes…there are some classed as *Jūnzǐ* who have not attained *Jén*

Yen Hui: And how would you define *Jén*?

Confucius: It is to love others quite simply

Tzu-kung: How about helping the many
by ameliorating their lot – can this be called *Jén*?

Confucius: Well..the man of *Jén* desiring to be established himself,
seeks also to establish others:
and the goals he wishes himself to attain,
he helps others to gain.
The Way of Humanity, is to be able to see others
by rule near to oneself.

Yen Hui: In other words the man who has attained *Jén*,
in any assertion of his claims,
only acts after recognizing others claims.

Confucius: That indeed is the way of the man of *Jén*

Tzu-kung: Pray is there a single word to act as a guide
for one's whole life?

Confucius: ***Reciprocity*** - what you do not wish to be done to you,
do not do to others.
Reciprocity is the ability to project one's feelings into others,
and to see the world from their point of view.

Tzu-kung: So *Jén* is the self-realization of man in society?

Confucius: Most decidedly!
Jén requires that, when at ease in your home you find yourself,
you should be circumspect:
in office you should show others respect:
in association with others, offer loyalty and sincerity,
and even though you with the barbarians be,
you will not forsaken find yourself.

Yen Hui: Tell us Master
in your opinion,
has any leader
ever come close to practising *Jén*?

Confucius: In recent times the only
that had an abundance of charity
and was full of consideration
for the plebeian population
was Tzu Chan of Cheng.

Yen Hui: And how did Tzu Chan of Cheng
manifest his charity?

Confucius: He assented to discussions of his policies freely[80]
and being a most magnanimous statesman,
he recognized in politics the right of freedom of expression.
His only short-coming was that he
did not countenance interference in foreign policy.

Yen Hui: And pray why did he arrive at such a conclusion?

Confucius: He argued that the plebeian
is carried away by haste and emotion
to policies which court catastrophe
for in seeking to make a name for himself instinctively,
he loses sight of the interest of the state and its citizenry.
For him only the nobleman
was fit to pronounce on affairs of the nation
which required reason.

Tzu-kung: So his idea of the *Jūnzǐ* was closely associated with the nobleman

Confucius: Indeed! He was predisposed to an understanding of the nobleman
as possessing innate superiority...

Though he was right in assuming the *Jūnzǐ*'s superiority
laying where matters of right are concerned
and the *Xiǎorén* where profit is concerned.
The distinction for me
rests on the possession of or lack of morality.

Yen Hui: So the difference between men is as regards morality
rather than of birth or in any powers of reason and intelligence?

---

[80] In the local district school

Confucius: Exactly! For only the very stupid and the very wise
cannot change their guise.

Tzu-kung: So there are innate differences of intelligence
which do not stem from either position or nativity?

Confucius: Yes - but I have yet to encounter
a man with insufficient power
to apply himself for a whole day to *Jén*.

Tzu-kung: So provided one has the necessary determination
anyone may attain *Jén*?

Confucius: Indeed even both of you one day may
achieve *Jén*'s Way.

(Confucius smiles and jokes)

By nature akin are men:
it is only practice that creates gaps between them:
moral sense is an inherent quality,
in which there is only minor distinction
and it is through acquired tuition
that there develops a difference of any degree.

Yen Hui: So Tzu Chan saw the distinction
between the *Jūnzǐ* and *Xiǎorén* as stemming
from innate power of reasoning,
which for him was to be found in the noble classes' possession,
whilst for you the difference rests in moral intelligence -
a difference that can arise with acquired training and guidance?

Confucius: Yes…Through instruction the *Jūnzǐ*
realises virtues' inherent goodness and beauty,
whilst the *Xiǎorén* in his ignorance cleaves to the soil selfishly.

Tzu-kung: Pray explain further Master…

Confucius: While the majority of people cling forever
to the rural society in which they first breathed their life,
the *Jūnzǐ* must part from this narrow and confining village society,
and in the environment of a broad and enlightened political society,
live a life of unfettered activity.
Thus if a *Jūnzǐ* clings to an idle and retired life,
he is not a fit person to bear the name of *Jūnzǐ*.

To regard knowledge as knowledge simply
and to know just this, is insufficient plainly!
Only by its direct application into action
is there to virtue, knowledge's transformation,

Tzu-kung: Knowledge then is a stepping stone to humanity
And as such practical reasoning - *humanity,*
should be placed on a higher footing
than *knowledge* - pure reasoning?

Confucius: Quite so, *practical reasoning* is superior
to *pure reasoning* as the former puts into action the latter.

After they depart Yen speaks to Tzu-kung marvelling
at the comprehensiveness and yet elusiveness of Confucius' teaching

Yen Hui: Tzu, the more I strain my gaze up towards it,
the higher they above me soar.
The deeper I bore…
down into it,
the more solid they turn out to be.
I see them in front me,
but suddenly they are behind me.
Step by step the master leads me skilfully.
He has broadened with culture, me
and taught me the restraints of propriety.
Even when I want to stop,
I cannot stop.

Just when I feel I have exerted my all,
something rises up further,
standing out sharp and clear.
Even though I long to pursue it,
I can find no way of getting to it
at all…

Tzu-kung: Heaven with knowledge has endowed him certainly
He is a Sage truly.
An exhaustible source of wisdom is our Master
constantly our minds stimulating.
It would be hard to equal him in learning
or in his virtuous behaviour.

The Attempt To Reduce The Three Huan's Power

For a long period Lu did to the Northern League align
with Qin its de facto head, prime
but Confucius wished to make
from this confederation a clean break.

For Confucius knew
the Three Huan's autocratic grip on Lu
was partly due to them being able to bribe
Qin's six most influential families
and with such powerful families
on their side,
were able to dragoon the prince of Lu
who in face of such coercion little could do.

(Confucius discussing the foreign policy change with the Duke Ding)

Confucius: Sire, too long have we been the slaves of the Qin.
I think it would be better
were we to withdraw from the Northern League.

Duke: I understand your sentiment concerning Qin
However, that would be difficult given the power
and influence they wield
through the Three Huan.

Confucius: Exactly sire, the Three Huan
have Qin for many a generation been bribing
to prevent the ducal House from rising.
If we withdrew it would arrest their treachery.
Preventing them from relying upon the Qin openly!

Duke: A most interesting proposition,
with the change in our foreign policy position
no external power would find justification
for any meddling
in our internal power jostling.
Thus the power of the Three undoubtedly undermining!

Confucius: Indeed sire.

Duke: A most wonderful idea.

Confucius then embarked on a policy
to contain the Three Huan's political supremacy
Their influence depended greatly
on the might of their private military.

Though, the forces they had stationed permanently
within the walls of the capital
were not formidable;
The base strongholds of each family
placed at points in their domains that were vulnerable,
such as, Hou of the Shu-sun,
and Ch'eng of the Meng-sun
and Pi of the Chi were well fortified and nigh on impregnable,
containing a large garrison of military
with armouries stockpiled fully.

Thus if the mansions of the families in the capital city
were ever, to attack suffer
they would be able to send for fresh military cover
from their respective forts easily.

Confucius realized it was essential
to have these forts dismantled permanently
if he were to reduce the Three Huan's power seriously
but they could be not forced to give up coercively
by the Duke or any other high official.

He had to find a way
That would the Three Huan's suspicions allay
making them with their own hands, their forts to the ground raze.

Confucius: How am I to convince the Three
to dismantle their fortifications freely?

Confucius thought it best to approach K'ang-tzu,
the leader of Chi
the most powerful family of the Three,
and the de facto ruler of Lu.
If he could K'ang-tzu persuade
the others to follow would not hesitate.

Confucius: Sir, the recent rebellion
was quite disastrous in Lu's history
and nearly saw the Three distinguished families' annihilation
And it does worry me greatly....
How are we to prevent a future repetition?

K'ang-tzu: The only way imaginable
is to have men in our keep who are loyal...
but then again loyalty can be bought.

Confucius: Especially in these uncertain times it can be easily bought.

K'ang-tzu: Pray Master Confucius, do you have a suggestion?

Confucius: Well sir, as I see it, the problem stems from your fortification

at Pi, and those of the other families at Ch'eng and Hou.

K'ang-tzu: I do not quite follow....

Confucius: Well, the forts are nigh on impregnable
As they should be and therein also lies the trouble.
Should someone gain control of them,
it would be extremely difficult to dislodge them.

K'ang-tzu: Mmmm certainly an interesting observation
but what would be your solution?

Confucius: Well were you to dismantle the defensive walls
of the three forts
then, were someone their control to gain
it would be easy to offensively them regain.

K'ang-tzu: I dare say yours is an interesting proposition...
we have suffered most in Yang Hu and Kung-Shan's rebellion
but I doubt if the Shu-sun and Meng-sun would agree to such an action.

Confucius: Well sir, surely were the leading family of the Three
suggest and undertake such an action enthusiastically
the other families would follow and understand its necessity

K'ang-tzu: Well we shall see....

Thus it was that in 498 B.C. the Chi family
gave Tzu-lu their Steward the order
to begin dismantling the defensive walls
of the fortress at Pi.
At first the plan went smoothly,
for soon after
the Chi had dismantled the defensive walls
of their stronghold of Pi.
And the Shu-sun family
soon thereafter
began destruction of the defensive walls
of their citadel quite willingly.
However, there still remained the Meng-sun family
they argued that their fort at Ch'eng was a vital strategic base
near the border between Lu and Ch'i,
and was in fact akin to Lu's north gate,
destroy this and the invading Ch'i military
could easily plunder Lu's dominion.
Thus to demolish it would be a foolhardy action.

(Confucius at Duke Ding's palace)

Duke: The Meng-sun are proving an obstacle
with their refusal.
Confucius: Indeed sire, though they do have a case pointedly,
for were they to demolish their fort's defences completely
it would leave it open to attack from the north by the Ch'i.

Duke: What action do you propose?

Confucius: Well, I would strongly urge you to lead a force
and by Ch'eng besieging
you could by military might enforce its dismantling.
The other families will not offer opposition
as each has already dismantled its fortification
and would not wish the Meng-sun family
to gain military ascendancy.

Duke: I am sure they will their action be regretting
but at the same time would not want to see
from their ill-judgement, the Meng-sun profiting.

Confucius: Most decidedly!

And so the Duke led a force
against the Meng-sun fort
but the defences at Ch'eng were most sturdy
The investing force
tried several times storming the fort.
Pegged back each time they retired unsuccessfully.

Having failed in his endeavour
to wrestle free from the Three Huan, power
Confucius lost their favour
and fell from position of political power.
Disappointed at this failure
he did not his ill luck, hope abandon
and in the following year,
forsaking his native Lu that he held so dear
commenced to various kingdoms his peregrination.
In almost every state
the rightful princes
had been ineffective made,
and in their places
ruled an oligarchy of families
from the aristocracy.
And though in Lu from the Three Families
Confucius had failed to wrest control free
he hoped to restore these other princes' standing
and create a society based upon respect and well-doing.

(Act XI) - The Years of Wandering
(497 BC)

The places under Confucius' rule were flourishing,
And crime began declining.
When news of this reached the people in Ch'i,
It worried them greatly
Afraid that should such success be replicated throughout Lu,
It would strengthen Lu internally
Such a Lu would prove an ally most attractive externally
And the neighbouring states would towards it gravitate
Then Lu the surrounding area may come to dominate
Such an eventuality the Ch'i could never come to be
So they schemed to prevent such an eventuality.

They decided to morally corrupt the ministers of state
away from matters of state
by sending eighty beautiful girls at the height of their nubility
and one hundred and twenty-five of the best horses in Ch'i
as a gift to Lu they hoped to tempt them to lapsing
into a life of hedonistic pleasuring.
Things came to pass as wished the Ch'i,
the Duke and the Barons of Lu ignored their government duties
so they could spend time with the young ladies.
The Duke and his ministers indulged in revelry.

They failed to hold a court meeting for three days in a row.
Disgusted by what he saw
in addition realizing that he was used rarely
in government in any great capacity
Confucius resolved to set off on his travels.
Although he was nearing the age of 60
accompanied by a handful of his disciples
amongst who were Tzu-lu and Yen Hui he left Lu promptly
in search of a wise duke who he could persuade
to following the Way.
For 13 years his peregrinations
took him to the in various Chinese nations.
He first made his way
to Lu's north-western neighbour Wèi.
After a short stay
to Sung, Cheng, Ch'en, Ts'ai did he make his way.
Then again through Wèi
back to Lu, to his final days pass away.

Wèi[81]

(Tzu-lu in conversation with Confucius in the carriage on the way to Wèi)

Tzu-lu: Sir, what if the ruler of Wèi wishes you to become part of his entourage.
What will be your first task?
Confucius: The language's rectification.[82]

Tzu Lu: Why do you place on it such high premium?

Confucius: If language is not used correctly,
then what is said won't be understood.
If what is said is not understood,
then the work of the state cannot be carried out successfully.
If the work of the state cannot be carried out successfully,
then the rules of propriety will not be observed and music [that is, culture] will not develop.
If propriety does not prevail, and if music [that is, culture] does not develop,
then criminal punishments will not be imposed in accordance with justice.
If criminal punishments are excessive
then the people disoriented in their actions will be
Therefore, the Jūnzǐ must see to it that language is used correctly
and that what he says, is in practice carried out correctly.

(On arriving at the capital, Duke Ling of Wèi received him with distinction)

Confucius at Duke Ling's Court

Duke: Come in Master Confucius…it is a pleasure
to meet such a distinguished figure.

(Confucius bows)

Confucius: His Majesty is most gracious in His praise
to one so humble.

Duke: Nonsense! I do not indulge in false praise
You are a sage most notable.

(Confucius appreciated, feels at ease)

---

[81] Simplified Chinese 卫 – original Chinese 衞
[82] Rectification of names

They say you are well versed in the art of government.
Tell me, what is the whole-mark of good government?

Confucius: Good government consists in the ruler being a ruler,
the minister being a minister,
the father a father
and the son a son.

Duke: And what of the prince?

Confucius: The prince....
Well when his personal conduct is correct,
his government is effective without the issuing of orders.
If his personal conduct is not correct,
Nobody will follow his orders!
But if his desire is for good,
the people will be good.

Duke: I see, and what if the personal conduct of the prince is lacking
......in say....moral integrity?

(He smiles as he thinks of his hedonistic life-style)

Confucius: In that case he should be sufficiently discerning
to appoint ministers who are virtuous and worthy.

This answer pleased the Duke for although he was given to his pleasures, he however did have at his disposal virtuous men as ministers

Duke: Indeed Master Confucius, if one lacks political acumen
one should appoint honest and loyal individuals
rather than corrupt officials
whose silver tongued ingratiation
seeks self-gain only.

Confucius: Sadly this is too often true Majesty

Duke: Tell me Confucius what in Lu was your stipend.

Confucius: Sixty thousand bushels of grain sire.

Duke: Well, as of today you shall be entitled to the same stipend
as part of my court here.

Confucius: His Highness
is most generous.

Nan-tzu
(On Virtue)

Soon Confucius was a regular at the Duke's court
and was perceived as being a threat to the officials of the court.

In particular the Duke's wife Nan-tzu,
A lady of great beauty and notoriety,
said to dabble in political conspiracy,
became afraid of the influence the old man from Lu
may come to wield upon the Duke's thinking.
So summoned she Confucius, for a meeting.

Nan-tzu sent to Confucius the following message:

When any gentleman from another nation
with friendship our lord does honour,
they always to me also pay a visitation
This is why Confucius I would like to meet you in my private chamber.

(Confucius at first declined but was then forced to accept)

Nan-tzu sat behind a transparent linen curtain
Confucius faced north and bowed on entering
She returned his bow from behind the curtain
With the jewels on her sash jingling

Nan-tzu: Tell me Master Confucius, do you believe there to be
any beauty over the ages of compare to me?

She steps from behind the curtain alluringly
And Confucius sees her manifest beauty.

Confucius: I am afraid Majesty
I am not well versed on the fables of physical beauty.

Nan-tzu: I see… I guess it is no mystery
that a sage has little time for …PAssions and …Beauty?

(She gazes at Confucius coyly)

It is said that the qílín[83] appears on the birth of a sage
although I must confess to never having seen one…thus far…
It is also related that on the chest of a sage
seven apertures there are,
would you be so kind as to satisfy my curiosity
and let me your chest see….

(Requesting in a most gentle alluring tone)

Confucius: I am afraid, of such strange phenomena
I have no knowledge.
I am no sage but of knowledge
a humble transmitter..

Nan-tzu: Now now…Master Confucius, modesty…
does not behove one of a wise and virtuous nature.

Confucius: You are most kind Majesty…
I am of knowledge and virtue but a lover.

Having failed Confucius, with her beauty to him captivate,
by appealing to his senses she tries him to fascinate.
She has her servants bring in seven kinds each
of rare incense, elixirs and meat.

Nan-tzu: Please, do these special delights savour
for I have chosen them in your honour,
and your opinion of their flavour me offer.

Confucius: I am afraid Majesty, being a coarse character
I am not used to such luxuries
my palate is poor equipped for such fineries,
as such I must decline your offer.

---

[83] 麒麟 is a mythical hooved Chinese chimerical creature known throughout various East Asian cultures, and is said to appear in conjunction with the arrival of a sage. It is a good omen that brings *ruì* (瑞); roughly translated as 'serenity' or 'prosperity'. It is often depicted with what looks like fire all over its body. It is sometimes called the 'Chinese unicorn'

Nan-tzu: You are indeed strange and quite rude…
such disrespect to your superior you display
by refusing my hospitality!

Confucius: No disrespect was intended Majesty,
I just am unable such delights to appreciate
such luxuries would be lost upon my palate so crude.

Nan-tzu: You truly are a remarkable soul…
There are few men who to temptation do not fall.

Confucius: Virtue your Majesty is more to man than either fire or water.
I have seen men die from treading on fire and water,
But a man die from treading the course of virtue I have seen never.

Nan-tzu: And what is this virtue?

Confucius: To practice the five following constitutes perfect virtue:
gravity, generosity of soul, sincerity,
earnestness, and kindness.

Nan-tzu: And of what use are such qualities?

Confucius: Well Majesty one may accomplish a great deal with these qualities.

If you are grave, no-one will, with disrespect you treat.
If you are generous, win all will you.
If you are sincere, repose trust will others
in you.
If you are earnest, you will much achieve.
And kindness, this will enable you to employ the services of others.

Nan-tzu: My dear Confucius
these are mere trifles of the powerless
What use are they to a Duchess of power?

Confucius: Well your Majesty tis true you can simply people order.
However they will follow only out of fear.
A loyalty such as that, one can easily with money buy.
But just imagine unremitting loyalty
borne out of love purely
Such loyalty no money will be able to buy…

Nan-tzu: An interesting supposition
I might give it some consideration….

(She smiles at Confucius affectionately)

Confucius back in his quarters is visited by Tzu-lu,
who is most angry at Confucius' visit to Nan-tzu

Tzu-lu: Why did you visit that licentious lady Master,
knowing full well her immoral character!

Confucius: I had no choice Tzu-lu,
having declined her first request for an interview,
she would not accept no for an answer
and sent her guards to wait for me until I had time to see her.
If what I did was wrong, may Heaven crush me!
May Heaven crush me!

(Confucius at Duke Ling's court)

Duke: Tell me Confucius how knowledgeable are you in the art of war?

Confucius: I am afraid my knowledge only extends to government and ritual
I am not versed in the art of war.

Duke: So much the pity as we are having problems with the Jin as per usual.

Confucius: I am afraid I am unable to offer
any assistance sire.

On this note and hearing of the intrigue
against him by jealous court officials
Confucius deemed it best to avoid such troubles
So the next day he took his leave.

Further Trials and Tribulations
Imprisonment at K'uang (492 B.C.)

Thus he with his disciples after ten months stay in Wèi,
decided to the state of Ch'in make their way.
Before Confucius went south from Wèi,
he was for a time minded in Qin to stay,
but on the way west at a place called K'uang,
a ferrying point near the Yellow River
nearly ended in disaster.
He was attacked and beaten by the townspeople of K'uang
who mistook him for Yang Hu,
the tyrant of Lu.
Yang Hu once attacked K'uang
and treated its people most harshly.
They arrested Confucius and his students believing mistakenly
Confucius to be Yang Hu the despoiler of K'uang

(Huan Zhou the head of the K'uang mob speaks)

Huan Zhou: At last we have you,
you wretch most immoral!

Confucius: And who exactly have you?

Huan Zhou: You, you scoundrel!
You shall pay for all the misery
that you brought upon our town.

Confucius: I am afraid you have me at a mystery.
How I Confucius, who hath never before set foot in this town
could possibly have been responsible
for any harm upon its townspeople?

Huan Zhou: Confucius! So is that name
behind which you hide your shame,
you coward Yang Hu!

Tzu-lu: You surely are mistaken, this is our Master…
Confucius a man renowned for his wisdom and moral character!
How could you possibly mistake him for that reprobate Yang Hu?

Huan Zhou: You can't fool us! You lying curs!
Come men lets drag these animals
to the prison and kill them later
on arrival of the commander!

(The protesting Confucius and his disciples are dragged to prison)

Yen Hui: What are we to do Master,
these people blinded by their hatred and anger
are bent on revenge for Yang Hu's cruel behaviour?

Confucius: Have no fear my children,
since the death of King Wen,
is not the course of culture in my keep?

The Disciples: It is indeed

If it had been the will of Heaven
to destroy this culture,
it would not have been given to a mortal for keeping.

But if it is the Will of Heaven
to prevent this culture
from perishing,
then what can these people do to me?
Have a little faith… we shall be free.

After a week's incarceration
The company was freed from their detention
after the commander of K'uang did return
and told them they had been mistaken.

Trials and Tribulations Continued…
Huan T'ui

Confucius abandoned his plan to Qin enter,
and turned south towards Ch'u's direction,
the Southern Alliance's leader
But again, before he could reach his destination,
Huan T'ui, a high noble of that state
tried to waylay and him assassinate.

Huan T'ui was a member of a powerful family in Sung
and a spoilt aristocrat of the worst sort.
A favourite of Duke Ching of Sung,
he exploited this fact to other people's property extort
until one day this resulted in him being soundly thrashed
As to defend himself or to retaliate, courage he lacked.

Nevertheless he remained in favour with the Duke
even though his arrogance alienated many high officers from the Duke
But, it was not until **484 BC**
that he began to fall from grace.
And finally in **481 BC**
the Duke tried him to assassinate
and so Huan and all the other members of his family
had to from Sung flee.

One of Confucius' disciples, Ssu-ma Niu
Was Huan T'ui's younger brother.
The complete opposite of his elder
a most kind and noble soul was Ssu-ma Niu.

After the whole family left their beloved nation
He refused in the same state to stay
with Huan T'ui.
On one occasion
he lamented that he 'had no brother,'
As Huan T'ui he did not a brother consider.

Confucius taught Ssu-ma Niu that true nobility
for him depended
on the mind and the spirit, not one's pedigree.
A man's worth depended
on what he was, not on his grandfather's authority.

These new set of values clashed strongly
with the conduct of Ssu-ma Niu's family,
and he could not suppress a sense of foreboding.
Confucius to console him uttered the following:

'If, within your heart when you see
you nothing wrong there discover,
then you have nothing to worry
and certainly nothing to fear.'

It was for this reason that Huan T'ui saw Confucius
as an influence most poisonous
turning his brother's mind against his elder
and so he against Confucius held a personal vendetta.

Tzu-lu: Master it was inexpedient of us this way to journey
through Huan T'ui's territory
given the enmity between him and Ssu-ma Niu,
which he firmly believes is due to you.

Min-sun: I must say I have to agree with Tzu-lu Master.

Confucius: My children have no fear.

If Heaven gave life to the virtue in me,
what harm can this Huan T'ui do to me?
Let us separate and change to the garbs of the common people
we shall be from them indistinguishable.
Under the cloak of night we shall leave
and by morn at that hill-top meet.

And so it was the company
Separated and passed unnoticed by Huan T'ui's military
who mistook them for the local citizenry.
So at the break of day we find the company united and happy.

Min Sun: Thou art indeed conducted with Heaven's mission,
We passed them by without allaying the slightest suspicion.

Confucius: My children.. how could that wretch, us kill
in wake of Heaven's will?

The company then made there way towards Ch'en,
travelling through a land almost barren,
with little food to scour for they did survive
on a diet of wild fruits, vegetables and the like.
As they camped one night parched and hungry
Tzu-lu rather resentful thus spoke angrily

Tzu-lu: Are there times when even the *Jūnzǐ*
is brought to such extreme straits?

Confucius: It never does surprise the *Jūnzǐ*
to find himself in dire straits.

Whilst the *Xiǎo Rén* finding himself in extreme difficulty
would throw over all restraint immediately.

Tzu-lu: I fear though Heaven has saved us from Huan T'ui's men
It will leave us to starve to death for the vultures to feast upon.

Confucius: My dear Tzu-lu
Heaven did not us from that scoundrel deliver
to die here in the wilderness of hunger.
Have faith…for I do….

Tzu-lu: I have faith in you Master
but when one is so weak with hunger
to keep faith is not easy

Confucius: Only through extreme straits is a true *Jūnzǐ* proved truly

The following morning as they travelled a while more
and a stream to their delight, they saw
with the sweetest most refreshing elixir
to quench their thirst, they had experienced never.
On they travelled until they reached Ch'en finally
in an extremely weakened state hungry.

They arrived at a time when Ch'en was making military preparation
for the inevitable invasion
by its powerful neighbour Wu.
Though Confucius and his companions were welcomed cordially
the Duke of Ch'en had no time to listen to creating a government of virtue.
He was interested only
in defending his kingdom from being annexed by Wu.

On Filial Piety[84] & Government
(489 BC)

After a few years of trying
to convert the Duke and his ministers to his thinking
he gave up and headed with his disciples to Ts'ai
for the Duke of She had requested Confucius' audience,
a man renowned for his virtue and good governance.
The Duke was overseeing the annexation of Ts'ai
by the powerful state of Chu
whose expansionist desire, few bounds knew.

Whilst travelling to their destination
the company came across a weeping lady
beside a grave,
and inquired the cause of her grieving state.

Confucius: My dear child what misery
has come to afflict you so profoundly?

Lady: Alas! My father-in-law was here by a tiger killed;
after that, my husband the same way perished;
and now my son did death the same way encounter.

Confucius: Then, why do you not move to a place that is safer?

Lady: The government here is not severe.

Confucius: There …a lesson for you all to remember!

(Cries he, turning to his disciples)

To endure life under bad government
is worse than threat from any tiger!

Tzu-lu: Indeed Master,
Governments can be most cruel in their treatment
towards their citizens than any beast could ever be.

(The company ride on)

---

[84] Xiào - 孝

Min Sun: Tell us Master what quality
should a good government official possess?

Confucius: Tell me what difficulty can one possess

in carrying the affairs of administration
if one is able to correct oneself?
But if a man cannot govern himself,
what business has he with others' regulation?
Was it not Shun who may be said to have done little
yet ruled successfully?
How did he manage such a miracle?
He corrected his person merely
and assumed his proper position
as ruler of his nation.

Min Sun: I take it he did not abrogate,
all his princely responsibilities of state
but merely left the daily administration to his ministers,
but of course he had to choose worthy ministers.

Confucius: Indeed, a wise ruler is he
that promotes the upright and worthy.

Tzu-lu: Tradition has it that Shun, choosing from the many,
elevated Kâo-yâo the virtuous as his Chief Minister,
whereupon the wicked fled the country.

Confucius: He truly was a most righteous Minister.

It was Kâo-yâo who first enunciated the importance
of the ruler pursuing the course of his virtue for good governance
which can be seen through his choice of official,
who will secure the repose of the people.

Thus did he mention:
'If the sovereign pursues the course of his virtue sincerely,
the counsels offered to him will be wisely,
and harmonious will be the aids he receives of admonition

Yen Hui: And pray what is the course of virtuous behaviour?

Confucius: For Kâo-yâo there were nine virtues in conduct to discover:

affability combined with dignity;
boldness combined with sincerity;
valour combined with righteousness;
mildness combined with firmness;
bluntness combined with respectfulness;
docility combined with boldness;
straightforwardness combined with gentleness;
aptness for government combined with reverent caution;
an easy negligence combined with discrimination.

Surely, when these qualities are displayed continuously,
Do we not have an officer most worthy?

The company finally make it to Ts'ai their destination
and after a day's relaxation
Confucius the Duke pays his visitation.

(In the Duke's private chamber)

Duke: Ah! Master Confucius…please do enter
It is an honour to have one so wise here

Confucius: My Lord is most gracious.
It is a pleasure to meet finally
a lord renowned for virtue and humanity.

Duke: You are most kind Master Confucius
I hope you had a trouble-free journey?

Confucius: It was quite straight-forward thankfully.

Duke: It is said on good government you are an authority.
Pray express your opinion on this matter freely?

Confucius: Government is good when it makes its citizenry happy
and attracts those who live far away.
Duke: Quite so, a happy and content people far more loyal stay
then those who out of fear display loyalty

Confucius: Indeed, loyalty gained through threat and tyranny
never compares with love and respect gained through kindness and generosity
The prince if like a father loved his people as his children
they would show loyalty and respect for him in turn.

Duke: Sentiments with which I whole-heartedly agree
Loyalty borne out of love is most deep
And what views have you on morality…?
Among the upright men of my country
if the father were to steal a sheep
then his son…
will bear witness to his transgression.

Confucius: Our people's uprightness is unlike this.
The son and father,
screen each other.
For us there is uprightness in this.

Duke: But surely that cannot be right,
the son must be given commendation
for carrying out a most difficult action
out of obeisance to what is right.

Confucius: Filial piety is the root of all *Jén*,[85]
and the stem from which grows all moral instruction.

Our bodies, every hair and bit of skin from our parents
do we gain.
So how can we presume to cause them any injury or pain?
Few are those who are naturally filial towards their parents
and dutiful towards their elder brothers but are fond of opposing their superiors;
and it never happens that those who do not like opposing their superiors
engage in the creation
of civilian commotion.
The *Jūnzǐ* concerns himself with the root;
if the root is firmly planted, the Way from it does shoot .
Filial piety and fraternal duty
surely they are the roots of humanity.

---

[85] 'Virtue' means the five virtuous principles, the constituents of humanity: benevolence, righteousness, propriety, knowledge, and fidelity

In the Major Odes of the Empire
They the following utter:
Ever think of your ancestor,
cultivating your virtuous character.[86]
Thus, in serving one's parents a man may gently with them remonstrate,
but if seeing he has failed to change their way,
he should resume an attitude of deference and not them frustrate;
may feel discouraged, but not resentment display.

Duke: You have a case undoubtedly,
however, for me priority has to be given to what is right
even at the expense of breaking filial piety.
Dilute must we not Right
by allegiance to one's family.

Confucius: With respect My Lord, if one breaks the bond of loyalty
that stems from filial piety,
then one will undermine virtue's foundation.
Only if reverence and respect is to parents given,
can filial piety be extended by generalization to family,
friends, society, and the whole of humanity.

Duke: I am afraid we will just have to agree to disagree.

Confucius: We must indeed....

After a few days stay
the company make their way
once again to Wèi

(Tzu-lu and Confucius talking in the carriage)

Tzu-lu: The Duke asked me what kind of man is your Master,
I did not know how to reply to him however.

[86] Shi III, i, ode 1, stanza 6, p. 431. Mao 235

Confucius: Why didn't you tell him
he is the sort of man so happy
upon enlightening those for knowledge hungry
that hunger he forgets easily,
and so content in doing this is he
that his sorrows he forgets freely
and does not realize that old age is creeping up on him?

Tzu-lu: Wish that I had Master,
however you are unlike any other
and sometimes it is not easy
to sum a man of many a good quality.
Confucius: A lover of knowledge would have sufficed.

Tzu-lu: A pity I got tongue-tied.

Return To Wèi – (488 BC)

Wèi was in a most unhappy state.
K'uai-wai heir-apparent tried to assassinate
his step-mother the Duchess Nan Tzu'
For this deed he had hired his retainer Xi Yangsu,

One morning, when the prince went to pay his respects to Nan Tzu,
his retainer hid himself with a dagger,
behind a curtain in a corner of her chamber.
As the Prince carried on a casual conversation with Nan Tzu,
he made a sign with his eyes in the direction
of the shadow behind the black curtain
but the assassin did not budge from his hiding place.
He gave the signal three times but to no avail
Nan Tzu, noticed the prince's strange behaviour
realized someone was concealed in the corner of the chamber.
She let out a shriek and dashed off to the inner chamber.
Startled by her scream, the Duke came to her.
K'uai-wai tried to blame his retainer Xi,
but he and all his adherents to Qin did flee.

In Chin, K'uai-wai's cause was taken
by one of its contending groups of noblemen
and installed him, in a city in Wèi.
By the time Confucius was in Wèi
his son was in the ducal palace happy
whilst his father held an outlying city by force of military.
However, power in the state lay neither
in the prince nor the father but K'ung Yu a minister.

On this particular occasion, as on all other occasions,
the duke received him gladly,
but their conversations,
which were on act of peaceful government previously,
were now directed to warlike decisions.

(Confucius visits the Duke)

Duke: Come my dear fellow
it's been long since I last you saw.
I am afraid I am unable to offer the same hospitality
as you already know of K'uai-wai's treachery.

Confucius: It did pain me greatly to learn of your misery.

Duke: I am afraid my misfortune does not there end
my dear friend.
Now I have Huan T'ui's rebellion also to contend

Confucius: Huan T'ui! That ingrate most dastardly!
How quickly he forgets your hospitality
when he and his family with their life did flee
and you offered him sanctuary.

Duke: He is an immoral individual
moved only by motives personal.

I was contemplating a military expedition
on his rebellious stronghold - Poo.

Confucius: That coward needs to be taught a lesson
for his disloyalty that he will forever rue.

Duke: In an ideal world it would be so.
However, there is a threat that should I do so
my enemies such as Chin would come to his rescue readily
and overcome my present weakened military.

Confucius: In that case sire
It would be best to delay to a date later
when you are in better state militarily
Huan T'ui's punishment for his ill-gotten territory.

The Duke now being of an advancing age
tended to leave the task of governing to others,
and weary of Confucius' high-flown lectures
as such Confucius ceased to take centre stage.
While in this disappointed disposition
Confucius received an invitation
from Fu Hsi, a retainer of the Chao family
Chin's most influential nobility.
Fu Hsi was the castle of Chung-mou's Keeper
He was plotting to hand over the city to Wèi.
Confucius was ready to make to him his way.
But once more Tzu-lu did interfere…

Tzu-lu: Master, I have heard you say many a time
that when a man is guilty of a personal crime,
the *Jūnzǐ* will from him stay far away.
If you accept the invitation of this wrong-doer,
who is in open rebellion against his superior,
what will people say?

(But Confucius, with dexterity replies)

Confucius: Tis true on many an occasion I have so spoken.
But is it not also true that if a thing be hard truly,
it may be ground without being made thin easily;

and if it be truly white
steep it in black fluid though you might,
but black it shall turn never?
Am I a gourd so bitter?
Am I to be hung up out of the way of being eaten?

Nevertheless Tzu-lu's objection did change Confucius' mind
and he Fu Hsi's offer declined.
His relations with the Duke did not improve any further,
and so dissatisfied was he with his patron's behaviour
that he retired from the Court altogether.

However, the de facto ruler
The minster K'ung Yu did him honour
And on many occasions to his advice defer.
Though K'ung Yu was far from being an angel
Confucius however wished to remain influential
and affect the government's matters practical.
Thus he had no choice but to associate with such a figure
and try to temper his demeanour
and of those whose standards much below of the Jūnzǐ.
Confucius' disciples wished him rigidly to remain to rules true
and disapproved of his association with K'ung Yu
as he had usurped the Duke's authority
So he spoke thus, wishing to open their eyes to reality.

Confucius: When I talk with a man I am not answerable
for what he may do afterward.
Why be so severe and judgmental?
When I talk with a man I am not assuming responsibility
for his past actions.
K'ung Yu is diligent and fond of study,
and is not ashamed to ask questions
of those below him in title and position
He is the only ruler to have sought my opinion
and acted upon whatever I offered as a suggestion.

Can you not see that by me tempering his demeanour
I may be a force for good and change his behaviour!

Tzu-lu: But surely what is right
is right!
And what is wrong
is wrong!
Once one consorts with the likes of K'ung Yu
one becomes tainted with the same brush too!

Confucius: My children do you not understand it is our duty
to convert even the usurpers to the Way.
K'ung sought my advice, the only ruler to have done so.
He seeks knowledge sincerely
Do I not have an obligation to show him the Way,
if he requests so?

However Kung did test Confucius' patience on occasion.
He married one of Duke Ling's daughters
to cement his position
and forced a noble of Wèi to marry one of his daughters
by divorcing his wives
But when that noble continued seeing one of his favourite wives
he wanted to lead against him a small force of military
and Confucius' advice on the matter he sought earnestly

K'ung: Master Confucius I have a slight matter
which has caused me much distress lately
and was wondering if you may offer a solution.

I my daughter's hand in marriage to one of the nobility did offer,
however, this scoundrel continues to one of his concubines see.
My mind is to attack him and teach him a lesson.

Confucius: Well sir, it is hardly an unexpected matter
as you forced this nobleman to divorce his favourite companion.

K'ung: Maybe so but, how could he turn away from the daughter
of a High Minister much above his station!

Confucius: Sir, the nobleman is a man worthy of admiration,
as he has not forsaken his duty to a wife
who was divorced under your coercion,
as such he should be allowed to keep his wife.
I urge you against military action!

K'ung: I have to Master Confucius, she is my daughter
I cannot allow him to humiliate her!

Confucius: You too sir upon him brought much humiliation,
he has not neglected your daughter
by continuing to be with his former
whom he freely renounced never.
In that there is no humiliation.

Confucius disgusted by Kung's behaviour,
intending to leave Wèi,
he his carriage did order
Thereupon K'ung apologized asking Confucius to stay
Confucius did reconsider,
but at that point messengers from Lu came
inviting him to return to his native land again.
As he himself was of quite an old age
and his disciples were also of a ripe age
he did not wish any longer to stay
and so the company back to Lu made their way
to friends and disciples who eagerly
did him wish to see.
For whilst away, in Lu his disciples had been busy.

In 495 Tzu-kung had attended an important diplomatic conference.
And in 488 at yet another conference
Where a high official of the powerful state of Wu
had summoned Chi K'ang-tzu,
K'ang-tzu being afraid of assassination
sent Tzu-kung instead as head of delegation

who being extremely diplomatic carried off the incidence
without an immediate rupture in their alliance
Thereafter Tzu-kung continued to prove himself able and worthy.

Jan Chi'iu in **484** *then the Steward of the Chi family*
planned measures for defending Lu against invasion from Ch'i.
He goaded the three families into action finally.
He took control of the 'army of the left', personally
with Fan Ch'ih[87] *as his deputy.*
In battle one of Lu's armies was defeated and did flee
but Jan Chi'iu used his troops so effectively
that the invaders had to retire ignominiously.

It was in this year that Confucius was invited back to Lu
at the behest of many disciples of note and Jan Chi'iu.
Their old Master had now for a decade been wandering
constantly in vain the Way preaching.
The disciples who had chosen to behind remain
now longed greatly to see Confucius again.

[87] Who later became Confucius' disciple

(Act X) - Return of The Master

When Confucius' carriage did the outskirts of Qu'fu reach
amidst the shade of dust most deep,
many students came to respectfully wait
the return of their Master at the city gate.

Jan Chi'iu: Welcome Master…
How wonderful it is to you see…

Tzu-kung: We have awaited your return so impatiently
Too long has it been since your presence did us honour.

Confucius: My children you do this old man great honour
and have with your welcome touched him deeply.

I too have missed your presence greatly
And it gladdens my heart, to here you all see.

(They all mingle freely renewing old friendships enthusiastically)

After resting at home for a while
Confucius paid visit to Duke Ai that very night

Duke: Come in Master Confucius, it is an honour
to meet our most distinguished citizen finally.
I hope I did not disturb you unduly
by requesting your audience so quickly
after such an arduous journey
but to see you I was most eager!

Confucius: It is always an honour
to pay visit to one's prince sire.

Duke: Your wisdom is well-renowned in the four corners of Zhōu.

Confucius: My Lord is most kind to praise me so
However, I am but a lover of knowledge
and disseminate simply
what I have learnt to those who seek.

Duke: Nonsense! You are a veritable font of knowledge
and finally one is presented with the opportunity
to with you speak.

Confucius: To impart what little I know
to those who hunger for it so,
always gives me great pleasure
Sire…..

Duke: You have travelled extensively in many a foreign nation
pray what is your opinion
on securing the people's submission?

Confucius: If you govern with virtue in your heart truly,
like the north polar star you will be,
which stays in its place while all others around it revolve naturally.

Look no further for examples then the government of Kings Wen and Wu
as written down on the tablets of bamboo.
'Let there be men and the government will flourish;
but without the men their government will languish'.

Duke: And what does this mean precisely?

Confucius: With the right men the growth of government is rapid,
just as the vegetation's growth in the earth is rapid;
moreover their government might be called a rush that grows easily.
Thus the administration of government lies in getting men who are worthy.

Duke: Worthy?

Confucius: Advance the upright and set aside the crooked,
then the people will submit.
set aside the upright and advance the crooked,
then the people will not submit.

Duke: Mmmmm undoubtedly.

He smiles knowing Confucius' censure.
They talk for a while longer
and then the Duke to his chamber does retire.

When Confucius had barely settled back in Lu
the luxury loving Chi K'ang-tzu
devised a plan to increase taxes against his already
poverty stricken citizenry.

He asked Jan Chi'iu to ask for Confucius' counsel
hoping he would give it the seal of approval
for the government fee
that he did from him receive.

Jan Chi'ui: Master Lord K'ang-tzu is in urgent need of finances
to build Lu's army
and prevent further invasions into its territory
and has suggested raising taxes.

Confucius: My dear Jan, the citizens of our Lu
are already taxed severely
to support the luxurious life-style of K'ang-tzu.
This taxation is nothing to do with bolstering the military
and saving Lu from its enemies
but rather to fund his personal luxuries.

Jan Chi'iu: He was hoping for your support Master…

Confucius: My support, he should know me better.
I could never countenance any measure
that increases the hardships our people already suffer
in order to enrich the nobles further.

Jan Chi'iu: What am I to do, it is his desire?
These aristocrats are used to their life of luxury
and do not take kindly
to officials who against their will them lecture.

Confucius: You must convince him to the contrary.
A *Jūnzǐ*, helps those who are needy,
and not make the wealthy still richer.
One who follows the Way when necessary,
must resolve Right, to further…
The conscience of any government official is an authority higher
than the command of one's ruler.

Jan Chi'iu: I shall see Master…

Confucius: Remember Jan if a state is governed according to the Way,
poverty and obscurity are things to us embarrass;
and if it is not governed according to the Way
then it is shameful to have wealth and status.

There the conversation ended and Jan Ch'iu went back to report to Chi K'ang-tzu

K'ang-tzu: Well it was expecting much of Confucius,
still having paid his stipend for many a year
it would have been, of him gracious
to have given me his support on this matter.

What say you Jan?

Jan Chi'iu: The Master is an idealist….

K'ang-tzu: And what of you Jan?

Jan Chi'iu: I am a realist….

K'ang-tzu: Good, in that case the task of tax collection
shall be your firm obligation!

Jan not being a man to give up such a promising career agreed even though he knew he would face Confucius' censure When Confucius got to hear of this he disowned him with anger:[88]

A follower of mine is he no-longer!
Beat the drum, my children for all to hear
and set upon him freely;
I give you leave openly!

[88] Nevertheless, remained on speaking terms and Confucius never did anything to undermine Jan's position

Good Governance & The Ideal Officer

On a clear sunkist autumn's day
With the woods in colour ablaze
We Confucius' and his disciples discover
by the banks of the Zhuhui Rive)

Confucius: Truly Nature's beauty
in autumn is manifest clear.
Look around at the majesty of its colour
and the swift ripples in the river
Swept along by the force of the breeze.

Min Sun: Without doubt Master
Such warmth do they radiate.
Truly Nature
does perfection create.

Confucius: If only Man could perceive the essence of beauty,
His nature would towards virtue veer
Away from selfish behaviour
And towards filial piety

Through his selfless actions
And respect and desire to establish his fellow Man
He would gain great satisfaction
As true pleasure he would experience and understand.

Tzu-lu: But few aspire to such responsibility

Confucius: Unfortunately…..

Tzu-chang:[89] Master, in what way should a person in authority
act in order that he may conduct government properly?

Confucius: Let him observe the five excellent things,
and banish away the four bad things,
then he may conduct government properly.

---

[89] One of the later disciples (48 years younger the Confucius) from the state of Chen, skilled at ritual but prone to excess and overly concerned with externalities

Tzu-xia:[90] And what five excellent things aid government properly?

Confucius: When the person in authority
makes more beneficial to the citizenry
the things from which they derive benefit naturally -
is not this being beneficent without great expenditure?

When he lays tasks on the people that are proper
who will then be malcontent and opposition him offer?
When on benevolent government his mind is desirous
who will then accuse him of being covetous?

When dealing with few people or many,
or with great things or small,
he does not dare to show any disrespect at all-
is not his called verily
maintaining a dignified ease without being haughty?

When he looks dignified and dresses properly
so that he is looked at with wonder.
Is not this to be majestic without being severe?

Tzu-chang: And what of the four bad things that government hinder.

Confucius: To put people to death without having instructed them properly
this is called cruelty.
To require from them all of their work suddenly
without having given them of this any caution
this is called oppression.
To at first issue orders as if without urgency
but when the time comes to insist on them with severity
this is called injury.

And, generally, in giving pay
or rewards to people,
in a mean way
is called acting the part of a mere official.

---

[90] One of the later disciples (45 years younger - renowned for his learning, cultural refinement though of somewhat cautious disposition) and now governor of Qu'fu

Confucius: As an official do not be desirous to have things done quickly;
do not look at small advantages.
Desire to have things done quickly prevents their being done thoroughly.
Looking at small advantages
prevents great affairs from being accomplished properly.

Tzu-xia: And what would you classify as good government?

Confucius: An effective government
must have food that is sufficient,
weapons enough to defend from invasion,
and confidence of the common citizen.

Tzu-kung:[91] Suppose that one of these three had to be dispensed with,
which should it be?

Confucius: Then weapons let it be.

Yen Hui: And what if one of the remaining two has to be dispensed with
Which should it be?

Confucius: Then food let it be.
For, of old,
death has been men's lot;
but if the people have no confidence in the government
the state cannot long itself maintain.

Tzu-kung: I take by this you do not mean that a government
should starve its people.. in order to itself maintain
but that rulers should not drive and exploit their people
for the sake of economic gain,
while giving the excuse that it is '*for the good of the people*'?

Confucius: I do not. The state should be viewed as a cooperative enterprise
in which all, the rulers and the ruled alike,
share in the understanding of its purpose proper
and the enjoyment of its economic gain together.

Tzu-kung: What qualities must a man acquire
to entitle him to be a government officer?

[91] Now in the Chi family's diplomatic commission

Confucius: He who in conduct maintains a sense of honour
and when sent to any quarter
will not his leader's commission dishonour,
deserves to be called an official proper.

Tzu-kung: May I venture to ask who may be placed in the next rank lower?

Confucius: He whom, the circle of his relatives pronounce to be filial
and whom his fellow-villagers and neighbours pronounce to be fraternal.

Tzu-kung: And how about the class still next in order?

Confucius: Those who are determined to be sincere
in what they do and utter.
They are obstinate little people.
Yet perhaps they, the next class may make.

Tzu-kung: Of what sort are the present day's people,
who in government engage?

Confucius: They are nothing but misfits and bunglers
not worthy for one to consider.

On Heaven

(Confucius atop Nang Hill with Hui, Tzu-lu, and Tzu-kung)

Confucius: Truly a view most Heavenly!

Tzu-lu: Such beauty …truly!

They all take in the majestic scenery
And feel like they gods

Tzu-lu: Tell me Master how best may one serve the spirits?

Confucius: You cannot yet adequately serve the living..
How would you best serve spirits?

Tzu-lu: Master your tongue on occasion can be most unforgiving.

Well… then enlighten me a little of death?

Confucius: As yet you do not know what there is to know about life
Why should you want to know about death?

Tzu-lu: As always elusive you remain on the designs of the afterlife!

Tzu-kung: And on Heaven's Will what have you to say?

Confucius: I wish I had nothing to say!

Tzu-kung: But if our Master you say nothing
then we your disciples
too will have nothing
to hand on to others?

Tzu-lu: Is there something you wish not to us reveal?

Confucius: Do you think there is something I from you conceal?
I nothing from you conceal.

But, surely does Heaven speak?
The four seasons in their turn come to be,
Every living thing comes to be
Yet does Heaven have anything to speak?

The Final Years

His last years Confucius spent rearranging
the anthology of poetry[92]*,*
and to teaching
as at this time he had students many.
Although Confucius from public office was in retirement
He continued to influence affairs of government
through those disciples in government.

Thus, when Wèi's Duke Ch'u
fled and sought refuge in Lu,
Jan Ch'iu and Tzu-kung sought Confucius' direction
as to the attitude toward him to be taken.
He continued to remain on terms friendly
with the head of the Chi family.
And intervened personally
in the murder of the Duke of Ch'i.

A son of the Duke of Ch'en
Two centuries previously,
fled to the state of Ch'i,
their ruler received him kindly
He founded in Ch'i the Ch'en family,
taking the name from his native Ch'en.

The Ch'en family became prominent nobles of Ch'i .
They installed themselves in the populace's favour
by distributing their largess freely.
Its members also became involved in political conspiracy
and began removing one after the other
the families that stood between them and control of Ch'i.

In 489 BC they were deeply implicated in the Duke's murder
and set a puppet the Duke Tao in his position situate,
who proved rather difficult to manipulate
and was murdered in mysterious ways four years later.
His son the Duke Chien's supporters did plan
to expel the Ch'en clan
and in 481 BC the Chen forestalled this by revolting
and the Duke killing.

---

[92] The Book of Poetry (*Shī Jīng*)

At this juncture Confucius proposed intervention.
Ch'i, was Lu's great northern neighbour,
which had kept the small state in subjection
and made war upon it, for many a year.
For the ruthless Ch'en to rule Ch'i
was not in the interests of any party.

Confucius hearing of the turmoil in Ch'i
went, the Duke Ai to see.

Confucius: My Lord, I urge you to take action
against the murderer Ch'en Heng.

Duke: Lu has been kept in a weakened condition,
How could it possibly take on the powerful Ch'en Heng?

Confucius: Ch'en Heng has murdered his ruler,
half of the people are against the Ch'en family,
if the army of Lu be added to one half of the Ch'i,
we can it conquer.

Duke: I am not in a position
to carry out military action!
You need first the Three Huan to agree
and then Lu can proceed with an attack on the Ch'en family.

However The Three Huan were unwilling to take action
and so nothing came of Confucius' suggestion
Once more disappointed he did from public affairs retire
But soon much pain and sorrow he had to suffer.

Confucius' Sorrows

First in 482 BC, he lost his only son Kong Li
and then his favourite disciple Yen Hui in 481 BC

Confucius: *Alas! Heaven has bereft me!*
Heaven has bereft me!

Among my disciples it was Yen Hui,
who the greatest desire for learning did display
With a single dish of rice a day
with a gourd dish of drink to keep hunger at bay,
whilst living in a hovel, so filthy,
conditions others could not have endured such misery.
You did not allow your pleasure in life to be affected
by such a state most wretched!

Only you truly did comprehend
that the search for knowledge and for Jén
was in fact identical with the search for a happy life.
Few are those who comprehend
that the highest of pleasure
in knowledge and learning one cannot discover,
but only when one reaches the state of Jén
is there also attainment of a happy life.

Confucius filled with sorrow bewailed Yen exceedingly,
whereupon, his disciples did come to worry.

Tzu Kung: Sir! You are carrying your grief to excess.

Confucius: Have I gone to excess….?
But if I may not grieve
over this man, for whom shall I grieve….?
Even under circumstances of great poverty,
Yen found in his love of learning self-sufficiency.

When death did Yen Hui take
his family being of an extremely humble state,
could not afford to give him a great funeral.
The disciples proposed to give him an imposing funeral
but Confucius refused to countenance any such spectacle.

Yen Lu:[93] Master I beg you your carriage to sell
in order that I may obtain for my son's coffin an outer shell.

Confucius: Every one calls his son
his son,
whether he has talents
or has not talents….
Li, when he died, had a coffin but no outer shell.
I would not walk on foot to get for him a shell,
because having followed in the rear of many a great officer,
that I should walk on foot it was not proper.

Tzu-kung: But Master surely
Yen Yuan is most deserving, of a funeral great?

Confucius: That my children would be utterly
in bad taste!

Tzu-lu: Master I beg to with you disagree
A man such a Yen deserves a funeral most stately.

Confucius: It will not do. Hui!
You regarded me as a father,
while I am not permitted to regard you as my son proper.
But it is not I, but my disciples erring way.

The disciples disregarded their Master's protest
And followed Yen Hui to the grave with profound respect
With Confucius a forlorn figure most lonely
Following, consumed in his grief completely.

In the same year an officer who controlled a city
in neighbouring state of Little Chu came to Lu,
Seeking certain guarantees he offered to annex his city to Lu.
Such agreements were commonly sworn with a treaty.
But he did not wish for such a treaty,
instead he merely requested a gentleman's agreement with Tzu-lu.
Tzu-lu refused and thereupon Chi K'ang-tzu
sent Jan Chi'iu to persuade Tzu-lu.

---

[93] Yen Hui's father

Jan: My dear Tzu-lu,
how can this be a disgrace to you,
since he will not trust the sworn covenant of a great nation,
yet puts in your mere words great conviction.

Tzu-lu: If Lu should go to war with Little Chu,
I should go to war with Little Chu,
I would die before its capital willingly
without asking the reason for the hostility.
But he is a traitor
to his ruler;
to treat him as an honest individual,
is that of which I am incapable!

Jan: You can be quite obstinate sometimes Tzu-lu.
Can you not see how advantageous this would be to Lu?

Tzu-Lu: Jan, when a man starts dealing with such a traitor
then he should seriously his morals consider.
I would be unable to keep my conscience clear.
You and Chi K'ang-tzu may do whatever you desire.
As for me you may inform Chi
that as from today I resign my services with his family.

Jan: Now… now my dear Tzu-lu.
You are over-reacting, isn't that true?

Tzu-lu: That as maybe Jan…
However, I can no-longer work for such a man.

(Tzu-lu along with his protégé Tzu-kao visit Confucius)

Tzu-lu: Master, I can for Chi K'ang work no-longer
and keep my conscience clear!

Confucius: My dear Tzu, one who is a great officer
serves his lord according to what is right,
and when he finds he cannot do what is right,
with his reputation untarnished does retire.

The *Jūnzǐ* in everything righteousness does first consider.
If, looking within he nothing does see
for which to rebuke himself he,
then what has he to fear?

Tzu-lu: True Master, but now I have work somewhere to gain
other than with the Three Huan who are all the same.

Confucius: I know of one who would welcome a man of virtue
such as you.

Tzu-lu: Who?

Confucius: The Minister K'ung of Wèi,
though he is far from being a saintly figure,
he certainly virtue, in others does admire.

Tzu-lu: Well he was rather kind to us while we were in Wèi.

The End

480 BC when he was very ill the well meaning Tzu-lu
lamenting the fact high office, escaped his Master completely,
had the disciples attire as ministers in attendance upon a high dignitary.
Confucius regaining consciousness scolded Tzu-lu

Confucius: By making this pretence of having ministers
when I have none, whom do you think I will deceive?
Shall I Heaven deceive?
Further, is it not better
I should die in the hands of my friends, most dear
than in the hands of ministers?

Tzu-lu: I am sorry Master, at least let me pray for you.
so that your passage to Heaven will be a smooth one.

(Confucius smiles)

Confucius: My dear Tzu
My kind of praying was long ago done.

480 BC Ssu-Ma Niu under mysterious circumstances passes away
Soon after Tzu-lu went to Wèi,
taking along Tzu-kao, his protégé.
They both entered the service of the K'ung family.
However, 478 B.C. Tzu-lu passed away tragically.
When rebellion broke and the K'ung family
was in serious jeopardy
Tzu-kao did make good his escape
and tried Tzu-lu to persuade.
'I have eaten their pay,
and will not flee from their misfortune this day.'
Did he respond and so trying his chief to defend,
struck down with dagger-axes he met his heroic end

When news of his death did Confucius reach in Lu
he was deeply saddened at the loss of his dear Tzu.

Confucius: My dear Tzu
There are very few
With your sense of honour and loyalty.
With you gone too, I have been bereft truly!

With the demise
of his son and dearest friends so suddenly
Confucius lost his appetite for life
And so in the 16th year of Duke Ai's reign in 479 BC
a day in the fourth month, at the age of seventy-two
after a week's sickness death relieved the Sage gently
Buried was he in the K'ung cemetery outside the gates of Qu'fu.

(Tzu-kung eulogizing Confucius at the funeral)

There is no greater wealth than wisdom;
no greater poverty than ignorance;
no greater heritage than culture.

They Way to wisdom and culture
Is long and arduous in nature
And takes many a year....

The Master said, at fifteen upon learning, I set my heart.
At thirty, I had planted my feet upon the ground firmly.
At forty, I no longer suffered from any perplexity.
I knew what the bidding of Heaven was at fifty.
I with docile ear I heard them at sixty.
At seventy my desire no longer overstepped the Right's boundary.
for I could follow the dictates of my own heart.

Like the North Star,
his effulgence shone the Way afar
for one and all
there was no guide truer his like before....

Free was he entirely
of any foregone conclusion,
arbitrary predetermination,
obstinacy or egoism.

Bereft us does he leave
of his knowledge and kindness
generosity and goodness,
his friendship and company.

Confucius' disciples at his grave did mourn him for years three
and Tzu-kung remained a further years three.